Cecilia Lucy Brightwell, C. L. Brightwell

Annals of Industry and Genius

Cecilia Lucy Brightwell, C. L. Brightwell

Annals of Industry and Genius

ISBN/EAN: 9783337117801

Printed in Europe, USA, Canada, Australia, Japan

Cover: Foto ©ninafisch / pixelio.de

More available books at **www.hansebooks.com**

ANNALS OF INDUSTRY AND GENIUS

BY

C. L. BRIGHTWELL,

AUTHOR OF "ANNALS OF CURIOUS AND ROMANTIC LIVES,"
"ABOVE RUBIES," ETC.

"IN ALL LABOUR THERE IS PROFIT."—*Solomon.*

LONDON:
T. NELSON AND SONS, PATERNOSTER ROW;
EDINBURGH; AND NEW YORK.
1869.

IT cannot be otherwise than instructive for the young to study the life-histories of those who have distinguished themselves among their fellows, and attained the objects to which they have aspired in life.

Many obstacles must be overcome, and, in not a few cases, serious hindrances encountered by all who ardently long to acquire knowledge and to secure the prizes which are presented to the ambition of enterprising minds. There can, indeed, be no question that, from every profession, examples may be brought in which talent and industry have not secured success. But, generally speaking, the axiom of the Wise Man holds good, "The hand of the diligent maketh rich;" and the long labour of preparatory study, careful observation, and assiduous, conscientious effort, are crowned with the deserved reward.

In the biographical sketches here presented, the reader will find examples of those who have attained celebrity in the world by dint of industry and self-denial, in some instances coupled with an amount of natural genius not given to all. To *all* there is given this encouragement: that if they cultivate, with care and self-denial, the talents God has given them, they will have the approbation of their own consciences and the approval of those whose good opinion is worth having.

The important services rendered to general literature and science by some of the individuals mentioned in this little book, awaken feelings of satisfaction and pride; and the writer earnestly desires that her readers—and may their name be Legion!—may distinguish themselves some day for intellectual zeal and power, and deserve to be remembered for moral dignity of character, piety to God, and benevolence to man.

CONTENTS

	Page
John Ludwig, the Self-taught Saxon Peasant	9
Peter Nieuwland	22
Sir William Jones	29
Cervantes	46
Tycho Brahe	68
Tom Britton, the Musical Small-Coal Man	90
Giovanni Battista Belzoni	99
Dr. Alexander Murray	118
Benjamin Franklin	134
William Hutton	157
Joseph and Stephen Montgolfier	175
Philip Matthew Hahn	193
Robert Gooch	202
Christian Gottlob Heyne, Professor of Eloquence in the University of Gottingen	217
John Bacon	232
Louis Holberg	245
William Gifford	265
James Ferguson	284
Sir Robert Strange	301

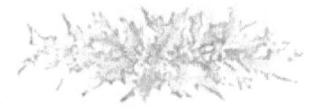

ANNALS OF INDUSTRY AND GENIUS.

John Ludwig,

THE SELF-TAUGHT SAXON PEASANT.

ABOUT the year 1753, one of the Commissioners of Excise in Saxony, named Hoffman, in the discharge of his duties, met with a somewhat remarkable individual. It was then the custom to appoint a peasant in each village to receive the excise of the place, and, as M. Hoffman was auditing the accounts of some of these people in the villages around Dresden, he was told that one of them, named John Ludwig, was a strange man, who, though very poor and with a family, was continually reading books, and frequently stood a great part of the night at his door, gazing up at the stars.

This account raised the commissioner's curiosity, and he desired that the man should be brought before him, which was accordingly done. The first impression produced by the appearance of the prodigy was unprepossessing;—a more rustic boor was never beheld; his hair hung down over his forehead into his

LUDWIG BEFORE THE COMMISSIONER.

eyes; his appearance was heavy and stupid, and his manners, in every respect, those of a plodding, ignorant clown. After surveying him, the commissioner inquired if what his neighbours had said about his studying and reading were true? "Who has told you that I study and read?" replied Ludwig; "that is my own affair; nor do I desire that you, or any one else, should know anything of the matter. If I have studied, I have studied for myself."

Not disconcerted by so rude and discouraging an answer, M. Hoffman managed to put a few questions with so much tact that he elicited replies, which convinced him the man was indeed a most extraordinary genius. Astonished at receiving from him such answers to the questions he put concerning arithmetic and the first rudiments of astronomy as would have done honour to a regular academic in a public examination, after this conversation he prevailed on the peasant to stay some time at his house, that he might have the opportunity of gratifying his curiosity with respect to a man who was so evidently quite self-taught. By degrees he won the confidence of his guest, and obtained from him a full account of his early history and his acquisitions.

"My name," said he, "is John Ludwig, and I was born in 1715, in the village of Cossedande, and when very young was sent together with several other poor children to school. The book by which I was taught to read was the Bible; and I was so much interested and pleased with this book that I eagerly desired to read others; but there was no other to be had, nor did I know by what means I could get any.

"In about a year my master taught me to write. At first I found this very irksome, but when I had surmounted the difficulty of forming the letters, I took to it readily enough, especially as books were then put into my hands to copy, as an exercise. When I was ten years old I began to learn arithmetic, but as my teacher would not trouble himself to explain the innumerable difficulties which I met with, but expected me to be content with the practice of positive rules, I was disgusted with arithmetic altogether, and after much scolding and beating, left the school without having learned anything more than reading, writing, and the catechism.

"I was then sent into the fields to keep cows, where I herded with boys of my own age, and learned to be as idle and clownish as they, thoughtless of everything except my daily task. The greater part of what I had learned was quite forgotten, and as I grew up I gave myself to evil habits, and tried to find satisfaction in vicious ways, and such amusements as were within my reach. Yet, all this time I had not lost the remembrance of the pleasure I once felt in learning, and I recollected that I had been praised by my master, and preferred before all my companions on account of my superior diligence and progress, and I wished I could again enjoy the same pleasures, but I knew not how to do so.

"At length, when I was about twenty years old I bought a small Bible, at the end of which was a catechism, with references to a great number of texts. As I had never been accustomed to take anything upon trust, I was continually turning over the leaves of my Bible to find the passages referred to, but finding this a troublesome task, I set about transcribing the catechism with all the texts at large, in their proper places. In this way I filled two quires of paper, and though when I began the characters were scarcely legible, before I had finished the task I found myself greatly improved. An art once learned, may be easily recovered.

"In the month of March, 1736, I was appointed to receive the excise of the district in which I lived, and I found it would be necessary for me not only to write, but to be master of the two first rules of arithmetic; addition and subtraction. I had now an object, and the desire I felt to keep my accounts in better style than others of my station, determined me, at whatever cost of labour, to apply to arithmetic. I now regretted I had not a teacher, and would gladly have practised the rules without asking questions. At last I recollected that one of my schoolfellows had a book from which examples of several rules were taken by the master to exercise the scholars. I found, to my joy, he still possessed this volume, and having borrowed it, I carried it home with me, beginning my studies as I walked along, and pursuing them so diligently, that in six months I was master of the rule of three with fractions.

"I now knew enough to make me earnestly desirous of knowing more; I was therefore impatient to proceed from this book to one that was more advanced, and having in some way found means to procure one

LUDWIG STUDYING ARITHMETIC.

which treated of more difficult and complicated calculations, I mastered that also, before the end of the year 1739. I had the good fortune soon after to meet with a treatise of Geometry, written by Pacheck, the same author whose arithmetic I had been studying. I applied with diligence to this new book for some time, but at length laid it aside, partly because I could not comprehend the theory as I went on, nor see the utility of the practice, but chiefly on account of the necessity I was under of immediately attending to my field and my vines.

"The severe winter we had in the year 1740, compelled me to keep closely confined in-doors for many weeks, and then, having no employment either for body or mind, I once more had recourse to the book of Geometry, and having at length comprehended some of the leading principles, I procured a little box ruler, and an old pair of compasses, on one point of which I mounted the end of a quill cut into a pen. With these instruments I employed myself incessantly in making various geometrical figures on paper, to illustrate the theory by a solution of the problems. I was thus busied in my cottage till March, and the joy I felt in the knowledge I had acquired was exceeded only by my desire of knowing more.

"But I was now again obliged to lay aside these studies, and betake myself to the labour by which alone I could earn bread. I was also without money to procure such books and instruments as were absolutely necessary to pursue my geometrical studies. However, with the assistance of a neighbouring artisan, I got the figures which I found represented by the diagrams in my book, made in wood, and with these I went to work at every interval of leisure, which now happened only once a week, after divine service, on a Sunday. I still wanted a new book, and having laid by a small sum against the time of the fair, which was the only opportunity I had of going to a bookseller's shop, I bought three small volumes, from which I acquired a complete knowledge of trigonometry. After this I could not rest till I had begun to study astronomy, and my next purchase therefore was an introduction to that science, which I read with unwearying interest, and invented a great many contrivances to supply my want of proper instruments.

"During my studies, I had frequently met with the word *Philosophy*, and this became more and more the subject of my thoughts. I supposed it was the name of some science of great importance with which I was, as yet, wholly unacquainted, and became exceedingly impatient to inform myself about it. Being continually on the look out, I picked up, at length, a book called 'An Introduction to the Knowledge of God, of Man, and of the Universe;' and in reading this I found much that was equally interesting and new. As however this treatise contained only general principles, I resolved to go to Dresden, and there I inquired among the booksellers who was the most celebrated author that had written on Philosophy? They recommended me to the Works of Wolfius, written in the German language, and I accordingly purchased his Logic, and at this laboured a full year, still attending to my other studies, so as not to lose what I had already gained. In this book I found myself referred to another, by the same author, called Mathematical Principles, and I therefore inquired about it, intending to buy it; but as it was too dear for my means, I contented myself with an abridgment of it, which I got in the autumn of 1743. From this also, I derived much pleasure and profit.

"I next proceeded to metaphysics, at which I worked for some months, and would fain have entered on the study of physics, but my poverty was an insurmountable obstacle, and I was obliged to content myself with this author's Morality, Politics, and Remarks on Metaphysics, which employed me till July 1746, by which time I had scraped together a sum sufficient to buy the Physics, which I had so earnestly desired, and this work I read twice within the year.

Shortly after, a dealer in old books sold me a volume of Wolfius' Mathematical Principles at large, and the spherical trigonometry which I found in this book was a new treasure of which I was eager to possess myself. However, it cost me incredible labour, and filled every moment I could spare from business and sleep for something more than a year.

"I next proceeded to the study of Kahrel's Law of Nature and Nations, and at the same time procured a little book on the terrestrial and celestial globes. These books, together with a few others I borrowed, are the sources from which I have derived the scanty stock of knowledge I possess."

Thus did this singular man describe the manner in which he had gradually acquired such an amount of information, as is seldom found even among those who have associated with the students of a University, and had perpetual access to public Libraries.

M. Hoffman, during Ludwig's residence at his house, dressed him in his own gown, with other suitable garments, and he observed that this alteration in dress had such an effect, that he could hardly persuade himself the man's accent or dialect were the same, and he even felt secretly inclined to treat him with more deference than when he wore his peasant's garb, although the alteration was made in his own presence, and with his own apparel.

It is probable that these effects also resulted from M. Hoffman's acquaintance with the true facts of Ludwig's history, which gave him a high idea of the man, and predisposed him to regard him more favourably. Besides which, it is not unlikely that intercourse with M. Hoffman softened the deportment of his guest, and rendered him, even unconsciously to himself, more courteous and gentle in manner.

It chanced that before Ludwig left, there was an eclipse of the sun, and M. Hoffman proposed that he should observe this phenomenon as an astronomer, and for that purpose furnished him with proper instruments. The impatience of the poor man while waiting for the eclipse is not to be described; he had hitherto been acquainted with the planetary world only by books, and had viewed the heavens with the naked eye alone. He had never yet looked through a telescope, and the anticipation of the pleasure which the new observation would yield him, scarcely allowed him either to eat or sleep. But it unfortunately happened that, just before the eclipse came on, the sky became cloudy, and continued so during the whole time it lasted. This misfortune was more than the philosophy of Ludwig could bear. As the cloud came on, he looked up at it in the agony of a man who expected the dissolution of nature would follow; when it passed over the sun he stood fixed in a consternation not to be described, and when he knew the eclipse was over, his disappointment and grief were little short of distraction.

M. Hoffman, in his turn, went soon after to visit Ludwig. He found him in an old crazy cottage, the inside of which had long been blackened with smoke. The walls were covered with propositions and diagrams, written with chalk; in one corner was a bed, in another a cradle, and under a small window at the side, three pieces of board laid side by side over two tressels, made a writing table for the philosopher, upon which were scattered some pieces of writing paper, containing extracts from books, various calculations and geometrical figures. The books which have been mentioned above, were placed upon a shelf, with

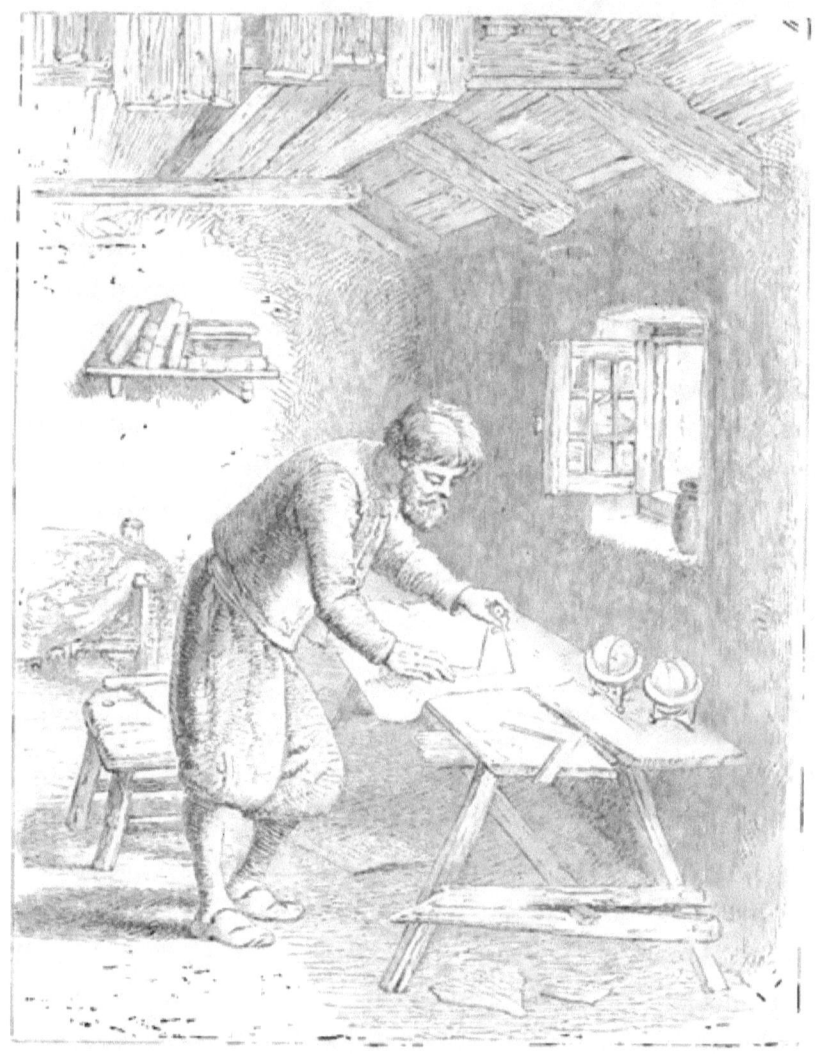

LUDWIG STUDYING GEOMETRY.

the compass and ruler that have been described, which, with a wooden square and a pair of six inch globes, constituted the library and museum of the truly remarkable John Ludwig.

In that hovel he lived till the year 1754, and while he was pursuing the study of philosophy in his leisure hours, he was indefatigable in his day labour, as a poor peasant, sometimes carrying a basket at his back, and sometimes driving a wheelbarrow, and crying such garden stuff as he had to sell about the village. In these circumstances he was subject to frequent insults, but he bore them without reply, or any mark of resentment and contempt, even when those who could not agree with him about the price of his commodities used to turn from him with an air of superiority, and call him in derision, a *silly* clown, or a *stupid dog*.

M. Hoffman, when he took leave of him, presented him with one hundred crowns, which abundantly gratified all his wishes, and made him the happiest man in the world. With this sum he built himself a more commodious habitation in the middle of his vineyard, and furnished it with many moveables and utensils of which he was greatly in want. But, above all, he procured a very considerable addition to his library, an article so essential to his happiness, that he assured M. Hoffman he would not accept the whole province in which he lived, upon condition that he should renounce his studies, and that he had rather live on bread and water, than deprive his mind of that food which its intellectual hunger perpetually required.

Peter Nieuwland.

PETER NIEUWLAND, Professor of Mathematics and of Natural Philosophy at Leyden, was born at Dierrmemeer, a village near Amsterdam, in 1764, and when young, exhibited very extraordinary proofs of genius. His premature death at the age of thirty cut short a career of unusual promise and talent; but limited as was his span of life, he effected much, and deserves to be held in honourable remembrance, both as a man of learning and ability, and as a Christian. His father, a master carpenter, was a man of sterling worth and good sense. He possessed considerable acquaintance with the practical parts of geometry relative to his profession, had well cultivated his natural abilities, and had accumulated a small library of instructive books. The good man was a member of the Lutheran Church, and had married a pious woman of the Baptist denomination, in whom he found a faithful helpmate, well-disposed to second him in bringing up their children in the nurture and admonition of the Lord.

Frequently this devout soul occupied herself in studying a family Bible, enriched with pictures, and occasionally as it lay open before her she would repeat the verses which were placed at the bottom of the engravings, and which she thus learned by heart, while her fingers busied themselves in some domestic occupation. She was greatly surprised one day to hear her little Peter, then three years old, lisping

NIEUWLAND'S INFANCY.

these same verses, while he pointed to the pictures that charmed his infant fancy. By the time he was five years old, he had read the whole Bible, and at seven, he was master of the contents of most of his father's books, and had made extracts from them of such passages as appeared to him most worthy of attention. Delighted with the wonders of natural history related in the travels which he had read, he wrote, at this early age, a poem in praise of the Great Creator, called "Orion," which was much admired by his countrymen, and gave indications of poetical genius. He received his first lessons in mathematics in his father's workshop, and soon manifested truly surprising talents for that science. He speedily outstripped his teacher, and at the age of eight years not only comprehended, but was able to demonstrate the theorem of the rectangular triangle. His father carried this young prodigy to the Professor Œnée, who put several difficult questions to him and received apt and unhesitating answers. This learned man having explained to him the formula of Newton's binomial theorem, the child of his own accord made the calculations relative to the elevations of the quantities to a given power, as soon as he had been put in the way to take the first steps. A surprising example, attested by M. Van Swinden, shows the ready skill of the young pupil. The professor asked him if he could determine the contents, in cubic inches, of a wooden figure which was placed upon a clock. "Give me a piece of the same wood," said the child, "I will reduce it to a

NIEUWLAND QUESTIONED BY THE PROFESSOR.

cubic inch, and then will compare its weight to that of the statue."

The construction of languages next occupied the attention of the young Nieuwland. Jerome de Bosch, a distinguished man of letters, instructed him. But the genius of the pupil was such, that he needed no more than to be acquainted with the first data, to seize upon the principles of the science. He seemed as it were by intuition to know the contents of a volume as soon as he had turned it over, and he would at once master a treatise, while casting his eyes over its pages. It was the same with languages; he studied first the construction of the mother tongue, and then, examining what the various idioms had in common and which distinguished them from the original, he was sufficiently conversant with them. In the same manner with the high mathematics; he calculated without ciphering, solely by his powers of comprehension. His imaginative powers were displayed in the composition of an entire poem, and his genius knew how to adapt itself to the poetical forms and the ancient writers. Before the age of eighteen he had translated with fidelity and spirit the most beautiful verses of the Greek and Latin poets upon the state of the soul after death.

The religious principles so early instilled into his mind by his excellent parents yielded the lovely fruits of virtue and modesty, and while his precocious talents excited admiration and surprise, his sweetness of temper and upright deportment secured to him, young as he was, the respectful affection usually reserved for men of maturer age. Although he must have felt his superiority, the ideas which he entertained of the greatness and glory of God, and his reverence for his masters, preserved him always humble, and he seemed to be even unconscious of his surprising powers. It is related of him that he was as devoted in his attachment to his native land as to the sciences he cultivated with so much ardour. He was invited by an influential man to settle in the United States, but he declined, fearing lest by accepting a valuable employment in a foreign country, he should deprive some worthy American citizen of his birthright. Nieuwland desired to find a happy home in his native land; and for a short season he tasted this felicity. He married an amiable and intelligent woman, but their union was shortly terminated by death. His wife, after giving birth to an infant daughter, expired at the age of twenty-two, and her child only survived her two days. The sensitive and poetic nature of the man rendered him most keenly alive to the anguish of bereavement. He vainly sought to soothe his regret by expressing his emotions in an elegy full of the most touching pathos. Unable to recover health and spirits it became necessary he should betake himself to a new scene of labour and observation.

He accordingly quitted Holland and established himself for a while at Gotha, with his friend, Professor Zach, in whose society he obtained some consolation, and with whom he applied to the study of astronomical science. Having made considerable progress in this new and absorbing branch of study, Nieuwland returned to Amsterdam, and resumed his former occupations. He now devoted himself to the belles lettres, and prepared an edition of the "Fragments of Musonius," in which he was engaged when the Admiralty of Amsterdam appointed him a member of the Commission for determining the Longitudes, and for the construction of hydrographic charts. His attention was consequently directed to the practical application of the science of astronomy.

In 1789 he was appointed Professor of Mathematics at the University, and filled that post during a period of six years, devoting his leisure to physics and chemistry. Before he had attained his thirtieth year he was called to fill the triple chair of physics, mathematics, and astronomy, at the University of Leyden.

Wholly absorbed in the various duties of his post, Nieuwland evinced the enlightened zeal of an old professor, united to the moral solicitude of a tender father for the numerous pupils who flocked to him from all parts. Beloved and honoured, he seemed destined to pass a life of usefulness in the instruction of those to whom his learning and piety presented so admirable an example. But it was otherwise determined by infinite wisdom, and Nieuwland breathed his last on the 14th November, 1794. His precise age was thirty years and nine days. He wrote several scientific works, a volume of poetry, and a great number of memoirs or treatises on various subjects.

Sir William Jones.

IT has been said with truth that resolute industry was one of the most distinguishing characteristics of this renowned scholar; and when reviewing the history of his life, we marvel no less at his unwearying application than at the excellent natural gifts with which he was endowed.

Sir William Jones was born in London, in the year 1746, of parents who deserve honourable mention. His father, William, was the child of a small farmer in the Isle of Angelsea, who gave his son the best education his narrow circumstances would admit of; and as the lad early addicted himself to the study of mathematics, he was sent, when young, on board a man-of-war, in the humble capacity of a teacher of that science. In this situation he so well conducted himself as to attract the friendly notice of Lord Anson; and on his return to England established himself in the metropolis as a teacher of mathematics, where, at the age of twenty-six, he published a work which was highly esteemed as a compendious but comprehensive summary of mathematical science. The private character and pleasing manners of Mr. Jones won for him the esteem and respect of his numerous patrons and pupils, insomuch that he reckoned among his friends some of the most eminent persons of his time. So highly were his merits appreciated by Sir Isaac Newton, that he prepared with his permission, and to his entire satisfaction, an edition of small tracts on the higher mathematics.

For a considerable period he resided in the family of Lord Macclesfield, at Sherborne Castle, giving instruction in his favourite sciences; and while there he became acquainted with Miss Mary Nix, the daughter of a cabinet-maker, who was a man of talents and manners so superior, that he was admitted on terms of intimacy to the society of Lord Macclesfield. This acquaintance resulted in a marriage, which promised to be productive of the truest happiness, but was speedily terminated by the death of Mr. Jones, who expired in 1749, leaving three infant children, the eldest of whom—William—was scarcely more than three years old. In consequence of this melancholy event, the family was left, with a very small fortune, to the care and management of the widow, who, being a woman of strong mind, good sense, and unusual accomplishments, devoted herself with diligence and skill to the performance of her arduous task. Perceiving the natural abilities and excellent disposition of her son, she determined to reject everything like severity of discipline, and to attract his young mind to the love of knowledge by making it pleasant to him. Exciting his curiosity, she answered his incessant questions by the invariable reply, "Read, and you will know"—a maxim to which he often referred, in after life, with gratitude. In his fourth year the boy was able to read distinctly and fluently any English book; and in his sixth he learned the rudiments of the Latin grammar.

An early taste for knowledge being thus instilled, he was placed, when seven years old, at Harrow school, where he was at first distinguished rather by his diligence than by his superior talents. His industry was soon rewarded by a more rapid progress, and in his twelfth year he was placed in the upper school, where the extraordinary powers with which he was gifted soon became apparent. So great was his diligence that he devoted to study many of the hours usually given to recreation, and his proficiency in consequence drew upon him the attention of the masters and the admiration of his associates. He was often flattered by the inquiries of strangers, under the appellation of the Great Scholar; and the then principal, Dr. Thackeray, gave it as his opinion that "Jones was a boy of so active a mind, that, if he were left naked and friendless on Salisbury Plain, he would, nevertheless, find the road to fame and fortune." So great was his ardour during the latter part of his residence at this seminary, that he frequently passed the night in study,

JONES PASSING THE NIGHT IN STUDY.

taking coffee and tea as an antidote to drowsiness, till at length, his eyesight being affected, such close application was forbidden. In the year 1764 he entered at University College, Oxford. To the extraordinary share of classical erudition which he had already acquired, he there added a knowledge of

Arabic, which he mastered by the assistance of a native of Aleppo, whom his zeal for study induced him to maintain at college, at an expense his finances could ill afford. At the same time he made a considerable progress in the Persic. His biographer (Lord Teignmouth) says, "At this period his vacations were passed in London, where he daily attended the schools of Angelo, for the purpose of learning to ride and fence. He was always a strenuous advocate for the practice of bodily exercises, as useful to invigorate the frame. At home his attention was directed to the modern languages, and he read the best authors in Italian, Spanish, and Portuguese, following in all respects the plan of education recommended by Milton, which he had by heart; and thus, to transcribe an observation of his own, "with the fortune of a peasant, giving himself the education of a prince."

In 1765 he accepted the situation of private tutor in the family of Lord Spencer, and in the year following was appointed to a fellowship in the university. In the family with whom he now resided he continued to pursue his favourite studies with unremitting eagerness, and when but in his twenty-first year commenced his celebrated Commentaries on Asiatic Poetry. He now formed several valuable friendships; and translated into French the "Life of Nadir Shah," from a Persian manuscript—a task which he undertook by the desire of the King of Denmark. In the year 1769 he accompanied his pupil on a continental tour; and shortly after his return to England, yielding to the solicitations of his friends, he determined to dedicate himself to the study of the law as a profession, and was admitted a student of the Temple. With characteristic activity and ardour he commenced his legal education, and we gain an insight into the amount of his labour and zeal in a letter addressed to one of his friends at this period,—" I have learned so much, seen so much, written, said, and thought so much since I conversed with you, that were I to tell half what I have learned, seen, read, said, and thought, my letter would have no end. I spent the whole winter in attending the public speeches of our greatest lawyers and senators, and in studying our own admirable laws, which exhibit the most noble example of human wisdom that the mind of man can contemplate. If I stay in England, I shall print my 'De Poesi Asiatica' next summer, though I shall be at least £200 out of pocket by it. In short, if you wish to know my occupations, read the beginning of Middleton's Cicero, and you will see my model."

In 1774 he gave to the world his "Commentaries on Asiatic Poetry," and in the end of the same year was called to the bar. We learn from his correspondence that he soon acquired considerable practice; and how sedulously he applied to the duties of his profession appears in the following extract from a letter dated July 1777:—"I would exert myself with great pleasure to comply with your friendly request, but the absolute want of leisure renders it impossible. My law employments, attendance in the courts, incessant studies, the arrangement of pleadings, trials of causes, and opinions to clients, scarcely allow me a few moments for eating and sleeping." In the meantime he continued his classical studies; and some idea may be formed of the range of his acquirements at this time from a memorandum, drawn up by him in 1780, in which he notes his intention of perfecting himself in twelve languages —Greek, Latin, Italian, French, Spanish, Portuguese, Hebrew, Arabic, Persian, Turkish, German, and English—as "the *means* of acquiring accurate knowledge of history, arts, and sciences, to one or other of which divisions every species of human knowledge may be reduced." At the end of that year he published a translation of the seven famous Arabic poems, and in the course of the two following years his celebrated essay on the Law of Bailments, and several pamphlets of a temporary and political nature.

The most interesting period of his life was now approaching. In March 1783 he was gratified by receiving an appointment to the situation of a judge in the Supreme Court of Judicature in India, an object to which his hopes and wishes had been directed from his first entrance into life, and which appeared to give him all the opportunities of personal advancement, as well as usefulness, which he had so long desired. Immediately on his nomination, he married Miss Shipley, daughter of the Bishop of St. Asaph, to whom he had been long attached, and in whose society he enjoyed true happiness. Accompanied by her, he embarked in April for that country whence he was never to return. During the voyage he addressed a letter to Lord Ashburton, to whose friendly offices he principally owed his appointment, in which he warmly expressed his gratitude, adding, "It is possible that by incessant labour and irksome attendance at the bar, I might in due time have attained all that my limited ambition could aspire to ; but in no other station than that I owe to your friendship could I have gratified at once my boundless curiosity concerning the people of the East, continued the exercise of my profession, in which I sincerely delight, and enjoyed at the same time the comforts of domestic life." It is with peculiar interest and satisfaction we find that, with the flattering prospect now opening before him, the thoughts and affections of Sir William Jones were not confined to the transient concerns of the present life only, but that he cherished an habitual feeling of piety in his heart, and lived in obedience to the divine will, and in humble anticipation of everlasting life through the merits of the Redeemer. Among many pleasing evidences of the religious feelings that prompted him, we find the following short prayer, composed on waking, July 27, at sea:—"Graciously accept our thanks, thou Giver of all good, for having preserved us another night, and bestowed on us another day. Oh, grant that on this day we may meditate in thy law with joyful veneration, and keep it, in all our actions, with firm obedience."

Minute circumstances often serve as indications of character. As an instance of this, we may mention the application made by him of two lines of Milton to his own case. He wrote them upon two of his cards, under his name; and they serve to show the frame of mind with which he looked onward to his future career,—

> "Not wandering poor, but trusting all his wealth
> With God, who called him to a world unknown."

On another scrap of paper among his notes were found the following lines, in his handwriting:—

> Sir Edward Coke.
> "Six hours in sleep, in law's grave study six,
> Four spent in prayer, the rest on nature fix."
>
> Rather.
> "Seven hours to law, to soothing slumber seven,
> Ten to the world allot—and all to heaven."

In the month of September the voyagers reached Calcutta, where the new judge was received with cordial congratulations by those to whom his reputation for talents and wisdom was not unknown. In the following December he entered on his judicial functions, which he thenceforward discharged with unwearying diligence and skilful discrimination, while the integrity that marked his conduct in the discharge of the solemn duties of his station was long remembered in Calcutta, both by Europeans and natives. His knowlege of the Sanscrit and Arabic eminently qualified him for the administration of justice in India; and his universal philanthropy and benevolence won general esteem.

In the year succeeding that of his arrival, a terrible attack of fever exhausted his strength, and threatened to destroy life. As soon as he was sufficiently recovered he undertook a journey to Benares, in the course of which the disorder returned, and brought him, as he himself believed, to the brink of the grave. Under the solemn impression of an approaching eternity, he resigned himself to the will of God, and thus expressed his feelings at the throne of the heavenly mercy:—"Oh, thou bestower of all good, if it please Thee to continue my easy tasks in this life, grant me wisdom to perform them as a faithful servant. But if thy wisdom hath willed to end them by this thy visitation, admit me —not weighing my unworthiness, but through thy mercy declared in Christ—into thy heavenly mansions, that I may continually advance in happiness by advancing in true knowledge and awful love of Thee. Thy will be done."

It pleased God to restore him; and he returned, with renovated health, to resume his official duties, and to engage in various literary and scientific pursuits. His application was incessant. In India his studies began with the dawn, and when his health was sufficiently confirmed, he devoted seven hours a day during four or five months in the year, to professional engagements; and during the vacations he gave his unremitting attention to a complete knowledge of India, which could only be obtained in the country itself, where it was not his intention to make a prolonged stay. He writes in the following striking manner of the work on which his heart was set:—" My great object, at which I have long been labouring, is to give a complete digest of Hindu and Mussulman law. I have enabled myself, by excessive care, to read the oldest Sanscrit law books, with the help of a loose Persian paraphrase; and I have begun a translation of Menu into English. The best Arabian law tract I translated last year. What I can possibly perform alone I will, by God's blessing, perform; and I would write on the subject to the Minister, the Chancellor, the Board of Control, and the Directors, if I were not apprehensive that they who know the world but do not fully know me, would think that I expected some advantage, either of fame or patronage, by proposing to be made the Justinian of India; whereas, I am conscious of desiring no advantage but the pleasure of doing general good." The astonishing and unremitting zeal of this exemplary scholar are, indeed, abundantly shown in those researches of which he gave the results to the world in his different publications on the philosophy and literature of the Asiatic nations. The principal sources of amusement of which Sir William availed himself, were the conversation of the Pundits, with whom he talked freely in the language of the gods (Sanscrit) and botany, in which latter pursuit he was greatly assisted by Lady Jones. As a proof of the kindly benevolence of his heart, the following passage from one of his letters is quoted:—"Could the figure, instinct, and qualities of birds, beasts, insects, reptiles, and fish, be ascertained without giving pain to the objects of our examination, few studies would afford more exquisite delight; but I never could conceive with what feelings a naturalist can occasion the misery of an innocent bird, because it has gay plumage, and has never been accurately delineated, or deprive even a butterfly of its natural enjoyments, because it has the misfortune to be rare or beautiful; nor shall I ever forget the couplet of Ferdausi, for which Sadi, who quotes it with applause, pours blessings on his departed spirit:—

> 'Ah! spare yon emmet, rich in hoarded grain,
> He lives with pleasure, and he dies with pain.'

Whatever name may be given to my opinion, it has such an effect on my conduct that I never would suffer the *cocila*, whose wild native wood notes announce the approach of spring, to be caught in my garden, for the sake of comparing it with Buffon's description, though I have often examined the domestic and engaging *mayana*, which 'bids us good morrow' at our windows, and expects, as its reward, little more than security; and even when a fine young *manis*, or *pangolin*, was brought to me from the mountains, I solicited his restoration to his beloved rocks, because I found it impossible to preserve him in comfort at a distance from them."

So much was the society of this excellent man valued and sought after, that he was subject to frequent intrusions upon his hours of leisure, and found it desirable, for the sake of carrying on his studies without interruption, as well as for the benefit of air and exercise, to choose a residence at Krishan-Nagar, a place where the soil was dry, and the air pure. In this favourite retreat he regularly allotted his time to particular occupations, and adhered scrupulously to the distribution on which he had fixed. From certain private memoranda of these private pursuits, it appears that a portion of time was devoted to the perusal of the Scriptures, and that the writings of our best divines engaged a large share of his attention.

Thus passed usefully and happily away some eight or nine years. The only drawback seems to have arisen from the debilitated state of his wife's health, which at length rendered it imperatively necessary that she should return to England. Her departure took place in December 1793, and the poignancy of the regret felt by both at separation was much softened by the hope of a speedy reunion, as Sir William hoped in the ensuing season to have discharged his engagements with the government of India, and proposed to return homeward by a circuitous route—through Persia—with intent to pursue his researches.

But Providence had otherwise ordained. One evening, early in April 1794, he prolonged his walk to a late hour, in consequence of which he complained of aguish symptoms, to which at first he attached no importance. His complaint, of which he had no apprehension, was, in reality, inflammation in the liver. The progress of the disease was unusually rapid, and terminated fatally on the 27th April. The account given of his last hours, by a personal friend, is full of melancholy interest:—" Sir William was at his old garden-house, and all the entreaties of friends could not prevail on him to come into town, or to suffer any body but his native servants to attend him. At length he consented that a medical man should be summoned. This was only, however, on the evening before he expired, when Dr. Hare is very sure he had a serious impression and apprehension of his approaching end. He lamented frequently that he had not gone to England, and said he had no object to keep him longer there. He had dismissed his moulvis and pundits some months, and he wanted no more that they could furnish. In short, he had brought his plans nearly to a close. Feeling himself drawing near his end, he intimated that the will of God must be done, although he submitted to take what was prescribed. Towards morning, on the 27th, he arose, and dressed himself, and after taking a little tea, desired his servants to withdraw. Probably, he then resigned himself to God, and committed his soul to the Redeemer, whom he confessed before men.

"I went early in the morning, and found only Ennis beside the body, who shed many tears. He lay on his bed in a posture of meditation. I took a candle, and dwelt for some minutes on every feature. His face was infinitely beautiful, and had an exquisite delicacy—a fineness and variety I cannot describe, though the idea is fixed clear and deep in my own mind. His mouth was speaking, his forehead impressive of awe, and strongly characteristic of the laborious and unremitting attention he devoted to the acquisition of knowledge."

In his intercourse with the Indian natives, Sir William Jones was condescending and conciliatory. He liberally rewarded those who served him, and treated his dependants with kindness. It is, therefore, no matter of surprise that the pundits who were in the habit of attending him, testified at a public durbar, a few days after his decease, their sorrow by shedding tears, which they could not restrain, for his death; while at the same time they were at a loss for terms in which to express their admiration at the wonderful progress he had made in the sciences they professed.

It may very naturally be asked, how within the short space of forty-seven years it was possible to acquire such varied and extensive knowledge of the arts, sciences, and languages as this remarkable man attained. This question has been thus answered by Mr. Jeffrey in his review of the life of Sir William Jones:—" From the very commencement of his career, he appears to have taxed himself very highly, and having in early youth set before his eyes the standard of a noble and accomplished character in every department of excellence, he seems never to have lost sight of this object of emulation, and never to have remitted his exertions to elevate and conform himself to it in every particular. Though born in a condition very remote from affluence, he soon determined to give himself the education of a finished gentleman, and not only to cultivate all the elegance and refinement implied in that appellation, but to carry into the practice of an honourable profession all the lights and ornaments of philosophy and learning; and extending his ambition beyond the attainment of mere literary or professional eminence, to qualify himself for the management of public affairs, and to look forward to the higher rewards of patriotic virtue and political skill."

The perseverance and exemplary industry with

which he laboured in the prosecution of this magnificent plan, and the distinguished success which attended the accomplishment of all that part of it which the shortness of his life permitted him to execute, afford an instructive lesson to all who may be inclined by equal diligence to deserve an equal reward. The more we learn, indeed, of the early history of those who have left a great name to posterity, we shall probably be the more firmly persuaded that no substantial or permanent excellence can ever be attained without much pains, labour, and preparation, and that extraordinary talents are less necessary to the most brilliant success than perseverance and application.

Cervantes.

MIGUEL DE CERVANTES SAAVEDRA, the renowned author of "Don Quixote," was born in the month of October 1547, at Alcala de Henares, a town of New Castile, but a few miles distant from Madrid. The family of his father, originally from Galicia, belonged to the same class of society in which he placed the hero of his romance, and their name is honourably mentioned in Spanish annals so far back as the thirteenth century. His parents, Rodrigo Cervantes, and Leonora de Cortina, were, by right of birth, gentle folks, though not noble. They were poor; and their children (two sons and two daughters) inherited little from them except a good name and honourable standing in society. Cervantes had an uncle—Cervantes Saavedra of Alcanzar—and he always adopted this additional name.

But little is known of the early life of this great genius. He himself says, in a poem written at mature age,—

"From my most tender years I loved
The gentle art of poesy;"

and while still a boy, he delighted in dramatic representations, and so great was his taste for reading, that he never passed a printed paper in the streets without deciphering its contents.

As soon as he was old enough, he went to Salamanca as a student at the University there, and remained for two years. He then returned to Madrid, and was placed by his parents under the tuition of Juan de Hoyos, a learned theologian who filled the chair of belles lettres in that city. He now acquired a taste for literary pursuits, and wrote, as he mentions, a vast number of romances or ballads, beside a pastoral called " Filena," which, he boasts, attained celebrity. "The woods resounded with her name," he says, "and many a gay song was echoed by them. My many and pleasant rhymes and the light winds were burdened with my hopes, which were themselves light as the breezes, and shifting as the sands." Happy young aspirant of the Muses! Fondly indulging in the sweet day-dreams of the hour, he, like the rest of us, enjoyed the brightness, and feared not the coming storms of life.

Joyous of nature, and adorned with the bright sparkles of innate genius, no wonder the young Cervantes charmed his instructor, who called him, " my clever and beloved pupil," and did his best to advance the interests of the gifted and favourite youth.

At the age of twenty-one, Cervantes quitted

Madrid, in the household of Cardinal Acquaviva, and accompanied that prelate who had been sent to the Spanish capital, as the Pope's nuncio, on his return to Rome. In those days the sons of poor gentlemen often commenced their career in the households of princely patrons, to whom they looked for favour and support; and it has been conjectured that the recommendation of the kind ecclesiastic, his master, and the talents of the young man, were the means of procuring him this chance for a start in life. Cervantes filled the office of camarero, or personal attendant upon his new master, and remained in his service for several months, visiting in his suite Valencia and Barcelona, and traversing the south of France, countries which he afterwards described in his works, and which he had no other opportunity of seeing. At the time when he went to Rome, the war between the Turks and the Venetians, which was declared in 1570, gave him an opportunity of embracing the profession of arms, of which he was not slow to avail himself. His taste seems to have disposed him no less to the profession of arms than to that of letters; and he boldly states that "there never has been an instance in which students have taken up arms, that they have not proved themselves to be the best of soldiers;" and in his opinion military courage and literary talent go well hand and hand. The dangers and hardships of war presented no insuperable obstacle to one by nature so courageous, ardent, and eager for adventure; and to the end of life he prided himself upon the valorous deeds of his youth, and recalled them with satisfaction to memory.

The cause in which Cervantes took up arms was one that appealed to the feelings of the Christians as opposed to the adherents of the false prophet. The Venetians, assailed by the Turks, implored the assistance of the princes of Christendom, and Pope Pius V. sent in consequence a force commanded by Marc Antonio Colonna. Under this general Cervantes enlisted and served his first campaign. During the following year greater efforts were made, and the combined forces of all parties were placed under the command of Don John of Austria, who went in pursuit of the enemy, and fought on the 7th October 1571 the celebrated naval battle of Lepanto. Great was the righteous indignation of the Christian combatants against their opponents, who had recently taken the isle of Cyprus, and after perfidiously breaking their negotiations, had tortured to death many of its gallant defenders. The fight was bloody and destructive on both sides, three thousand of the Christians being slain, and a much larger number of the Ottomans, for no quarter was given during the heat of the battle. The result of this action was for a time fatal to the power of the Turkish navy in the Mediterranean. It was accordingly celebrated with solemn thanksgivings and rejoicings, and the surviving commanders were received in triumph on their return. The great Spanish lyric poet of the age, Herrera, wrote some of his finest odes in commemoration of this renowned victory, but his greater compatriot could boast that his prowess had aided to procure it, and he said long after, "As my eye wandered over the smooth of the sea, it recalled to my memory the heroic exploit of the heroic Don John, when, aided by courage, and by a heart throbbing for military glory, I had a share, humble though it was, in the victory." He took, indeed, a very active part in the affray. During the voyage he had suffered from fever, and was not recovered when the action commenced. His commander, as well as his comrades, recommended him to remain quietly in his cabin, but this he refused to do, entreating rather that one of the most exposed posts might be assigned to him: His request was complied with. The galley on board which he fought distinguished itself greatly, and killed near five hundred of the enemy, and took the royal standard of Egypt, while Cervantes, exposed to the fiercest assault of the foe, received three arquebus wounds, one of which dreadfully shattered his left hand. He was four-and-twenty years old at the time this affair took place, and when age had silvered his brows, looking at his maimed limb, he exclaimed, "I would rather be again present in that prodigious action than whole and sound without sharing in the glory of it."

Sick and wounded, he was left after the battle in hospital at Messina, where he lay disabled for six months, but his military ardour was unabated, and in the following year he joined another expedition fitted out by the Chiefs of the League, and sailed, this time, to the Archipelago. He was present at the unsuccessful assault on the Castle of Navarino, and made one of the force which vainly attempted to succour Goletta. Of these disastrous events he has given a very striking account in the story of " The Captive," related in the twelfth chapter of Don Quixote. Upon the latter occurrence, he wrote a sonnet, commencing—

> Amidst these barren fields and ruined towers
> The bed of honour of the falling brave,
> Three thousand champions of the Christian powers
> Found a new life and triumph in the grave.

In the summer of 1575 Cervantes obtained leave to revisit his native country, from which he had been absent seven years, eventful years for him, during which he had seen much, and barely escaped with his life from the perils of the bloody warfare. It was natural he should desire and endeavour to obtain the preferment he so richly deserved. He had high testimonials in his favour, and Don John gave him letters to the King Philip, making honourable mention of his conduct at Lepanto, and begging that he might receive a suitable appointment. Such recommendations promised fair, and, full of joyful anticipations, he embarked in the galley *El Sol*, accompanied by his brother Rodrigo, who joined him at Naples, from whence they sailed on their return to Spain. But a cruel disaster awaited them, which dashed all their hopes, and doomed them to years of suffering. On the 26th September the galley was attacked by an Algerine corsair, and, after a brave resistance was captured, and all on board carried to Algiers, where the crew and passengers were sold as slaves. Cervantes fell to the share of Arnaut Mamu, a Greek renegade, one of the most energetic and prosperous of those lawless pirates who carried on the nefarious traffic of cruising for captives, whom they sold into slavery on the African coast.

It is scarcely possible to imagine a more frightful position than that in which Cervantes thus suddenly found himself placed. Happily, many interesting details of his captivity have been preserved, and they show so much sagacity, resolution, and magnanimity on his part as command our admiration and respect. Of the way in which the prisoners were treated at Algiers, the following account is given in the tale of "The Captive," before referred to:—"We were shut up in a prison-house, which the Turks call a bagnio, where they keep their Christian slaves, both those belonging to the king and to private persons, and also those which are called *El Almacen*, that is, who belong to the public, and are employed by the city in works that belong to it. The king's slaves, who are ransomable, are not obliged to go to the works as others do, except their ransom stays too long before it comes, when, to hasten it, they make them work and fetch wood with the rest, which is no small labour. I was one of them who were to be ransomed, and so I passed my life in that bagnio, with several other gentlemen of quality, who expected their freedom, and though hunger and nakedness might, as they did often trouble us, yet nothing gave us such affliction as to hear and see the excessive cruelties with which our master used the other Christian slaves: he would hang one one day, then impale another, cut off the ears of a third, and this upon the slightest occasions, so that often the Turks would own he did it only for the pleasure of doing it, and because he was naturally an enemy to mankind.

"Only one Spanish soldier knew how to deal with him, and his name was *Saavedra;* and because he did such things as will not easily be forgotten by the Turks, and all to gain his liberty, his master never gave him a blow, nor used him ill either in word or deed; and yet we were always afraid that the least of his pranks would make him be impaled, nay, he himself sometimes was afraid of it too; and if it were not for fear of taking up too much time, I could tell such passages as would divert and cause you much wonder."

It is evident that Cervantes here alludes to himself, and we have the testimony of others that he did not in the least degree exaggerate his deeds. In a History of Algiers, published by Diego de Kaedo, a Spanish ecclesiastic, in 1612, there is a long description of the sufferings of Cervantes and his companions, and of the surprising efforts he made to regain his liberty. His first attempt was so far successful that he contrived to escape from Algiers with several others, but they were betrayed by their Moorish guide, and compelled to return. Shortly after their recapture one of their fellow-prisoners was ransomed, and he took with him letters from the two brothers Cervantes to their father, which safely reached him. The old man immediately sold his small property, thus reducing his family to poverty for the purpose of redeeming his sons. Unhappily, the sum so raised sufficed only to purchase the freedom of Rodrigo, who was released in the month of August 1577. For Miguel there were in store three more weary years of captivity, during the whole of which he was incessantly plotting schemes for escape. Shortly after his brother's departure he contrived to get possession of a garden near the shore, wherein he caused a cave to be excavated, to which several Christian slaves, who had escaped from bondage, fled for refuge. It was a secure asylum, though dark and damp, and, of necessity, unwholesome. Here, for more than seven months the fugitives remained, never breathing the air of heaven except at dead of night, when they stole out of their dismal lurking-place for a short time. "Of what these men suffered while they remained in that cave," says Kaedo, "and

CERVANTES DIRECTING THE EXCAVATION.

of the bold enterprises hazarded by Miguel de Cervantes, a particular history might be composed." Many fell sick, all endured much misery, and were mainly supported by the firmness and providence of Cervantes, who provided for their sustenance, and at length contrived to hire a vessel, which was brought to the neighbourhood of the garden at midnight, on the 28th September. All seemed secure, when suddenly an outcry was made by some Moors who caught sight of the prow of the brigantine as she neared the shore, and instantly gave the alarm. The captives in the cave were not discovered at the time, but two days later were betrayed, seized, and secured. Alluding to this event, Kaedo says, "The governor's emissaries took especial care to secure Cervantes, who was the contriver of the whole scheme, and he adds, "Had this man's good fortune been equal to his courage, enterprise, and skill, Algiers would at this day have been under Christian rule, for to no less an object did his designs aspire."

The prospect of ransom money alone saved the prisoners, who were thrown into a loathsome prison, and subjected to various privations and punishments. Cervantes, as the ringleader, was treated with so much severity, that, as he afterwards said, " he learned in that school of suffering to have patience under misfortune." So true is it, that to great and noble minds, "Sweet are the uses of adversity."

Undaunted by failure, this heroic man determined to renew his plots on the first opportunity, and he gained over a Moorish slave, whom he persuaded to convey a letter for him to the Spanish governor of Oran, beseeching him to aid a scheme he proposed for liberating himself and three of his fellow prisoners. The letter was intercepted, and the slave shot; Cervantes sentenced to two thousand stripes, from the infliction of which horrid punishment he was only saved by the urgent intercession of the Christians in Algiers, and (as may be conjectured) by the influence which his own extraordinary bravery exerted on the minds of his Turkish owners.

Again and again the indomitable captive repeated his efforts to obtain that freedom after which he pined with unutterable longing. At length he succeeded in escaping from the bagnio and hiding himself in the house of one of his old military comrades, when the Dey made a public proclamation, threatening with death any one who afforded him refuge. On this Cervantes, refusing to endanger his friend, delivered himself up, and was threatened with immediate execution unless he denounced his accomplices, for it was reported and believed that he had aimed at raising the whole Christian population to revolt, and attempting, by their assistance, to get possession of the town of Algiers for the Spanish crown. With admirable constancy Cervantes refused to implicate any one; fear of instant death could not induce him to break silence, and an eyewitness, a countryman of the great Spaniard, exclaimed, as he related this noble conduct, that Cervantes deserved "renown, honour, and a crown among Christians." As for the Dey, he was heard to say, that "he only held his city secure while he kept that maimed Christian in safe custody."

The ransom of the captive was eventually effected

in the year 1580, through the intervention of the Fathers of Mercy, a religious order, instituted by Innocent III. as early as the twelfth century, for the liberation of Christian slaves out of the hands of the infidels. At first its labours were chiefly directed to the ransom of the prisoners taken in the wars of the crusades, but Africa became at a later period the scene of its labours, and there was a company of friars resident at Algiers as redeemers of slaves for the kingdom of Aragon. The price set upon Cervantes was an exorbitant one, his value being proportioned to the distinction he had earned by his strenuous resistance and indomitable courage. Efforts were made to collect his ransom in Spain, and his poor mother, now a widow, contributed her scanty mite of two hundred and fifty ducats, to which his sister added fifty more, the utmost their small means allowed. Finally, the sum of five hundred gold crowns was procured and paid, as is proved by the registry of Cervantes' liberation in the archives of the Order of Mercy, in which he is described as an inhabitant of Madrid, aged thirty-three, of a middle size, much beard, and maimed in the left arm and hand."

Early in the following year he landed in Spain; what were his feelings we may infer from many passages in his writings, in which he speaks of the excessive joy of restoration to freedom—"On earth," he exclaims, "there is no good like regaining lost liberty." Alas! he was poor, unknown, and friendless; his long captivity had completely effaced the remembrance of his former deeds, and he found himself destitute of all resources, compelled to follow the example of his elder brother, who had again re-entered the service.

As a volunteer he served in three successive expeditions against the Azores, and in the campaign of 1573, was present at the taking of Terceira, on which occasion Rodrigo distinguished himself greatly, and was promoted to the rank of ensign. This was the last passage of arms in which, so far as appears, Cervantes was engaged. In the following year he published his first work, a pastoral romance, entitled, "Galatea," in which the author personified himself and the lady of his affections, Donna Catalina y Salazar. Thus we find that love was the spur which first impelled this great genius to composition, and he did not sue in vain, for the lady was so well pleased that soon after the publication of the work, she consented to become his wife. They were accordingly married in December 1584. This union seems to have been a happy one; the bride was of a noble family, though greatly impoverished: her dowry was very moderate, and the whole property of her husband amounted to no more than one thousand ducats.

> "When Poverty enters the door, young Love
> Will out of the window fly,"

to prevent which disastrous result Cervantes had now to exercise his wits. Doubtless, the feelings of innate genius buoyed up his spirit, and he felt that he had within him the power to charm mankind by the productions of his pen. There was a bright up-bubbling life and energy of soul within, which never suffered him to repine, although, from first to last, throughout his career, he struggled with penury, want, and neglect. His noble spirit disdained to murmur, and preserved its buoyancy and genial gladness.

Among the various literary projects to which his mind was now given, he turned his attention to the drama, and wrote numerous pieces, which have all, with few exceptions, perished; although at the time, he says, several were received with favour. It became necessary to find some less precarious occupation for the support of his family, especially as his two sisters greatly depended on his exertions; and he considered himself fortunate when an opportunity occurred which enabled him joyfully to "lay aside the pen and relinquish play-writing." The post of assistant commissary for provisioning the Spanish fleet was procured him by the interest of a friend; and this appointment occasioned his removal to Seville, where he lived for several years in the discharge of its duties. But that it was not sufficiently lucrative to satisfy his necessities is evident; for in May 1590 he petitioned the king to give him the place of paymaster in New Grenada. Fortunately this request was not granted; but his funds and his expectations must have been very low to make him propose going to South America, "that last refuge and asylum of despairing Spaniards," as he himself styled it.

At length, in 1596, the purveyorship was abolished, and his office at an end, and Cervantes for some time earned a scanty livelihood by serving commissions as a mercantile agent. It is interesting and instructive to find the genius of the man turning to fruitful account even this plodding interval of his existence, spent amid the turmoils of the busy city. He found in the active life and varied pursuits of its inhabitants, an ample field for the study of human nature, and the materials for many of his tales were furnished him by incidents that actually occurred at Seville.

Strange and melancholy it is to learn that among the various annoyances inflicted upon this great man, was the accusation of fraud in the execution of his trust. Certain monies which passed through his hands were abstracted by a merchant with whom he transacted business. The guilty party fled, and Cervantes was arrested and kept in prison till he gave security for the repayment of the lost sum.

About this period of his life all trace of his proceedings has been lost. It appears that he quitted Seville in 1598, and some four years after he was at Valla-

CERVANTES COMPOSING "DON QUIXOTE."

dolid; but in what manner the intervening time was passed has not been ascertained. Having recourse to conjecture, his biographers suppose him to have found employment in the province of La Mancha; and there is an old tradition that he was imprisoned by the alcalde of a village in that district, and that he wrote the first part of his "Don Quixote" while in confinement. The accuracy with which he has described the country of La Mancha and the manners and customs of its inhabitants leaves little room for doubt that he must, at some period, have resided there. Certain it is that the first part of his renowned work was published in 1604, when the author had attained his fifty-seventh year. For a short time only it was unnoticed. The writer was unknown to fame—an obscure man, and poor. The very title of the book was censured and misunderstood; but it only needed to be known, and its success was immediate. The public read it with intense relish, and its fame quickly spread; so that in one year four editions of it were printed in Spain, and its renown presently extended to other countries. A pleasing anecdote has been preserved, which shows the general popularity which attended the publication of this gem of Spanish literature: King Philip III. was standing one day in the balcony of his palace at Madrid, when he saw, on the opposite bank of the Manzanares, a student earnestly engaged in reading a book. At intervals the reader looked up and burst into fits of laughter, clapped his hand to his forehead, and gave other signs of extreme mirth. "That man," said the king. "is either crazy, or he is reading the history of Don Quixote." On inquiry, the courtiers ascertained that the latter conjecture of the monarch was correct; the student was absorbed in the masterpiece of Cervantes.

Notwithstanding the enthusiastic reception of his book Cervantes still continued poor, and his very success excited the envy of a host of literary rivals, who annoyed and disturbed him with satires, epigrams, and critiques. He even relates that on one occasion, he had to pay a rial for a letter which was brought to his house, and which he had the mortification to find contained nothing but a silly and discourteous sonnet, speaking ill of "Don Quixote." No wonder he "grudged the rial infinitely."

On the removal of the court to Madrid in 1606, Cervantes followed it, and he continued to inhabit the capital during the remainder of his life. His worldly affairs were little if at all improved; but he still managed to support his two sisters and his niece, who, together with his wife and daughter, constantly resided with him. Between him and his eldest sister, Andrea, there had always been a warm attachment. In earlier days she had assisted to ransom him from captivity; afterwards, when she became a widow in straitened circumstances, Cervantes afforded her and her child a home under his roof. Thus we find his household composed of five women dependent upon his liberality and kindness. It is clear Cervantes had that predilection for women's society which so often characterizes men of generous and refined feelings.

With old age advancing upon him, he seems to have lost none of the spring and life of his earlier days. He occupied himself in preparing for the press several works which had been written at various times. His "Novelas Exemplares" (Moral Tales), were published in 1613, and were thought to increase his reputation as an author. In the preface he gives us an interesting portrait of himself:—"He whom you here see with a face resembling an eagle's, with chesnut brown hair, smooth and open brow, vivacious eyes, a hooked yet well-proportioned nose; with a beard now silver, but which twenty years ago was golden; thick mustachios and small mouth; ill-formed teeth, of which but few remain; a person between two extremes, neither tall nor short; of sanguine complexion, rather fair than dark; somewhat heavy about the shoulders, and not very light of foot;—this, I say, is the face of the author of 'Galatea' and of 'Don Quixote dela Mancha.'"

The "Novelas" were speedily followed by the "Viage del Parnaso" (Voyage to Parnassus), a satirical poem, directed against the false pretenders to the honours of the Spanish Parnassus. Not long after its publication there appeared a pretended continuation of "Don Quixote," written, under an assumed name, by a writer who indulged in a fierce tirade of invective and abuse against Cervantes. Our author, naturally disgusted and highly indignant, hastened to complete the second part of his "Don Quixote," which appeared at the end of 1615. In the introduction he has these memorable words:—"Poverty may partially eclipse a gentleman, but cannot totally obscure him; and those glimmerings of ingenuity that peep through the chinks of a narrow fortune have always gained the esteem of noble and generous spirits."

Not many months after the appearance of this his last published work, the health of Cervantes began to decline. Hoping to find benefit from the country air, he occasionally made an excursion to Esquivias, from whence as he was one day returning to Madrid, in company of some friends, he was saluted by a student, who, joining the party, began to converse with the great writer, complimenting him with many expressions of admiration. In the course of conversation, Cervantes acquainted the stranger that he was suffering from dropsy, and that he feared the disorder would speedily reach a fatal crisis; adding, "My life is drawing to a close; and if I may judge by the quickness of my pulse, it will cease to beat by next Sunday, and I shall cease to live."

On the 18th of April 1616, finding his malady greatly increased, he received extreme unction, and on the following day he finished the dedicatory preface to a work he was preparing for publication. About, for the last time, to lay aside his pen, he thus bade adieu to what he most loved:—"Now, farewell pleasure! farewell joy! farewell my many friends! I am ready to die; and I leave you, desirous of meeting you soon again, happy in another life."

Thus, calm and self-possessed, with resigned and cheerful spirit, Cervantes died on the 23d day of April 1616, aged sixty-nine. It has been noted as a curious fact that our own Shakespeare expired on the same day.

In conformity with his own desire, his remains were interred in the convent of the Trinitarians, situated in the Calle del Leon in Madrid, in which street he lived at the time of his death. The very place is now unknown; no stone, no tomb, no inscription of any kind, marks the spot where the ashes of Cervantes repose.

Tycho Brahe.

IT is impossible to read the history of this celebrated astronomer without feelings of admiration mingled with surprise,—Admiration for the genius of the man and for the energetic and resolute character which enabled him, in the pursuit of his noble object, to overcome the prejudices of his station and steadily to persist in his course; Surprise at the credulity which made him a dupe to the fallacies of astrology and caused him to cherish idle superstitions.

He was born on the 14th December 1540, at Knudstorp, the estate of his ancestors, a small lordship near Helsingborg, in Scania. His father, Otto Brahe, having a large family, Tycho was educated under the care and at the expense of his uncle, George Brahe, who, having no children, determined to adopt him as his heir. In the opinion of the aristocratic head of the family, the profession of arms was the only one suited for the scions of a noble race; and he accordingly resolved that his sons should be trained to it. Tycho, however, at a very early age,

TYCHO OBSERVING AN ECLIPSE OF THE SUN.

showed a decided aversion to the choice that had been made for him, and, with the connivance of his foster-parent, began the study of Latin in his seventh year, and continued it under the instruction of proper masters, from whom he also received occasional lessons in various other branches of knowledge.

When thirteen years old, the lad was sent to the university of Copenhagen, where he seems to have shown no fondness for any particular study; but when he had been there three months, an event occurred which first directed his attention to astronomy. This was a total eclipse of the sun, which it had been foretold was to happen on the 21st August 1560. Three hundred years ago, such a phenomenon was regarded in the light of a portentous sign, linked with and influential over the destinies of nations and of men. Tycho watched for its appearance with the curious eyes of youth; and when he saw the sun obscured and the heavens grow black at the very moment predicted, his admiration and astonishment were unbounded. He thought that science must be divine which could thus foresee future events and precisely tell the movements of the celestial bodies. This feeling is a very natural one; it is that which instinctively occurs to the mind of the uninstructed. Only the other day, on occasion of the recent eclipse of the sun, a Spanish peasant, expressing his astonishment at the precision with which the event was prognosticated, said, "I always knew there was one God; now I know there are many." On being asked his meaning, he said, "They must surely be gods who foreknew and could foretell all that!"

The young Danish student did not suffer his wonder to stifle his curiosity and inquisitiveness. On the contrary, he determined to make himself master of this surprising science, with which view he began to search with ardour such works as he could procure descriptive of the planetary motions. In 1562 he was sent to Leipsic to study civil law, but for this science he had no predilection; on the contrary, he disliked it, and made a running epigram upon it. Astronomy engrossed all his thoughts, and he spent the pocket-money allowed him in the purchase of astronomical books, which he eagerly read, secretly prosecuting his beloved study, and by means of a small celestial globe, "no bigger than his fist," he made himself acquainted with the positions and movements of the heavenly bodies. As his tutor continually remonstrated against pursuits which diverted his attention from the study of the law, he took the opportunity, whilst this mentor was asleep, to follow, night after night, the bright luminaries in their courses. The first instrument he used for observing the angles between the stars was a common compass, by the aid of which he discovered that the calculations of the Alphonsine and Prutenic Tables gave the places of the planets visibly wrong, and especially so in the case of the great conjunction of Jupiter and Saturn, which took place in August 1563. To this celebrated conjunction we are told Tycho gravely ascribed that great plague which in subsequent years desolated Europe, because it occurred in the beginning of Leo, and near the nebulous stars of Cancer; two of the zodiacal signs reckoned by Ptolemy "suffocating and pestilent."

Feeling his great need of better instruments, he now procured the assistance of an ingenious artist named Scultetus, who, under his directions, furnished him with what he required, and he was enabled to make a series of astronomical observations, some of which, dating from his sixteenth year are (it is said) still preserved at Copenhagen.

Having passed three years at Leipsic, he was preparing to travel through Germany when he was recalled in consequence of his uncle's death, to superintend the property which had been bequeathed to him. Thus restored to the companionship of his relatives and friends, Tycho might reasonably, as we should have imagined, anticipate kindliness and sympathy; but he found the very reverse. Rarely has the truth of the ancient proverb been more strikingly exemplified, "a prophet hath no honour in his own country." His kinsmen regarded with contempt his devotion to pursuits which they considered degrading for a man of birth and station, and reproached him for relinquishing his legal studies for what was, in their opinion, both useless and derogatory. There was but one honourable exception in the whole family. Steno Bille, his maternal uncle, applauded him for following the bent of his genius, and encouraged him to persevere.

Probably wounded by such ungracious usage, and desirous beside of prosecuting his travels, in a few months he again quitted his native country, with the intention of visiting the principal towns of Germany. He first proceeded to Wittenburg, from whence he was speedily driven by the terrors of the plague to Rostock, in which last place a fearful event befell him. He chanced to be invited to a wedding feast, where, among other guests, was a young Dane, named Pasberg, with whom Tycho unhappily entered into a dispute. They parted with feelings of mutual displeasure, and again meeting a few weeks later at some festive games, revived their former quarrel, and from angry words proceeded to blows.

Early one winter's morning these two intemperate youths met to settle their disputes at the point of the sword. They fought in total darkness, and in the blind combat a large part of Tycho's nose was cut off. In consequence of this disaster he was obliged ever after to wear an artificial one, composed of gold and silver, which was so skilful an imitation of nature that many, not acquainted with his loss, were completely deceived.

After having resided two years at Rostock he next paid a visit to Augsburg. This city was famous for its skilful mechanics, and our young astronomer had now the command of workmen who were capable of executing his plans. His genius soon displayed itself in the invention and improvement of various mathematical instruments, particularly an immense quadrant, so gigantic in size that twenty men could hardly lift it. It was constructed at the expense of the burgomaster, Paul Hainzell, who was an ardent lover of astronomy, and charmed with the grandeur of Tycho's plans. The best artists in Augsburg, clockmakers, jewellers, smiths and carpenters, were engaged to execute the work, which they did with so much zeal that in less than a month the quadrant was completed. With this instrument and a large sextant he also constructed, Tycho made many excellent observations during his stay at Augsburg. At the end of 1571 he returned to Denmark, and the fame which he had by this time acquired as an astronomer among the learned and distinguished men of Europe having excited general observation, he was invited to court, and loaded with attentions which were so many importunities to a man who hated ceremony, and longed for an opportunity to carry on his researches undisturbed. He therefore retired into seclusion, gladly availing himself of the offer of his excellent Uncle Steno, who invited him to his abode at the ancient convent of Herrtzvold, near to Knupstorf, where he provided him with commodious apartments and a suitable place for an observatory.

Not content with his astronomical researches, Tycho, at this period of his life, followed with no less zeal the study of chemistry or rather of alchemy, in the chimerical hope of enriching himself by its means. We have all heard of the philosopher's stone—that stumbling-block of sages—in the pursuit of this *ignis*

TYCHO DISCOVERING A STAR.

fatuus he now engaged, fitted up a laboratory, provided himself with furnaces, and all the requisite apparatus, and to a great extent forsook his sextants for his crucibles. An event, however, occurred in 1572 which aroused him from these fantastic pursuits and recalled his attention to the celestial orbs. On the 11th November, as he was returning in the evening from his laboratory, he chanced to observe the constellation of Cassiopeia, and was amazed at seeing there an extraordinary and unusual star, surpassing all the rest in splendour. Scarcely believing the evidence of his own eyes he immediately called out his servants and the peasants, who also saw it, and then, hastening to his observatory, he eagerly examined the brilliant stranger, noting its magnitude, light and motion. Chancing in the course of the ensuing spring to visit Copenhagen, he carried with him his journal in which he had inserted all the observations he had made on the new star and his conclusions from them. He soon found that the learned dons of the university were entirely ignorant of the phenomenon, and very sceptical as to his statements respecting it. Their scepticism was speedily exchanged for admiration and astonishment when they beheld with their own eyes the prodigy which Tycho pointed out to them at the first opportunity. Immediately they became urgent that he should publish his notes, which, however, he refused to do, on the pretext that the work was not sufficiently perfect, but the true reason, as he afterwards acknowledged, was that he considered it unbecoming his rank as a nobleman. Eventually these idle scruples were overcome, and his work on the new star appeared in 1573. This singular body continued visible during sixteen months, gradually diminishing in size. At one time it rivalled Venus in her greatest brightness.

Never were the prejudices of a man destined to be more completely broken down than in the case of this celebrated genius. Fearing to cast a stain upon his noble birth by publishing the results of his skill and observation, he next found himself compelled by the impulses of a loving heart to debase his lineage by marrying a plebeian girl of the village of Knupstorf, named Christiana. This was so serious an offence against his order that it excited the most intense indignation in his family. They thought themselves so much disgraced by this mis-alliance that they refused to hold any intercourse with the offender, until the king himself interposed and commanded a reconciliation.

For the rest, Tycho appears never to have repented his choice. His wife was beautiful, and he loved her. He preferred (he said) one who would be content without the ceremonious observances required by a woman of rank, and who would be satisfied to live in retirement, devoting herself to his society and finding her happiness in her family. His beloved Christiana realized his fond anticipations; she made him a good and dutiful wife, and was the mother of a numerous progeny. The reader will doubtless think Tycho had now secured a better treasure than the philosopher's stone, for in the words of the wise man, "He that findeth a wife, findeth a good thing, and shall obtain favour of the Lord."

Not long after this event he first appeared as a public teacher, and read lectures on astronomy at Copenhagen, by express desire of the king. Unhappily he not only gave a full view of the science of astronomy, but explained and defended all the reveries of astrology.

These affairs took place in 1573; and in the spring of 1575 he set out on a journey he had projected, leaving behind him his wife and infant child. His intention was to choose a place of permanent residence for his family. He first paid a visit to William, Landgrave of Hesse Cassel, who was himself an ardent patron of astronomical science, and noted for his skill and proficiency in making celestial observations. He then went into Switzerland, and at length fixed upon Basle as a home, the salubrity of the air and the celebrity of the university there offering him great inducements.

Returning into Denmark, he immediately prepared to transplant his family and effects; but while so engaged, was surprised at receiving the royal command to repair to the Court at Copenhagen as soon as possible. Obeying the summons, he was most graciously received by the monarch, Frederic II., who, having been informed of the intentions of his illustrious subject, and unwilling that Denmark should be deprived of so great an ornament, offered him a grant for life of the island of Huen, in the Sound, and promised to furnish him at his own expense with the requisite instruments, a house for his family, and a laboratory for carrying on his experiments. So munificent an offer was gladly and gratefully accepted, and Tycho lost no time in surveying his new territory, which he found admirably fitted for his purposes. The island of Huen is about six miles from the coast of Zealand, three from that of Sweden, and fourteen from Copenhagen. It is some six miles in circumference, rises gradually in the form of a mountain, and is a fertile and pleasant little ocean gem. The highest and central part of the island commands a noble prospect; on one side the coast of Zealand stretching far away, the shores gently sloping, richly wooded, and beautifully sprinkled with villages and villas; on the other side, the rocky and almost naked cliffs of Sweden, adorned with the spires of many distant towns; and to the north, a boundless expanse of ocean, covered with the vessels of various nations. On this elevated spot, in the heart of his domain, Tycho resolved to build a grand astronomical castle, to be called Uraniberg, or the City of the Heavens. The foundation stone of this edifice was accordingly laid on the 8th August 1576, the ceremony being performed early in the morning of a brilliant day, in the presence of a large party of nobility and gentry, assembled to do honour to the occasion. A full description of this magnificent pile is given by Gassendi, in his life of Tycho Brahe. The principal building was about sixty feet square; the apartments for the family were numerous and handsome; there was also a museum, with a library and a subterranean laboratory, and numerous other buildings. On the hill, a little to the south of Uraniberg, an observatory, called Steirnberg, or the Mountain of the Stars, was connected by an underground passage with the laboratory. These various buildings were erected in a regular style of architecture, and were highly ornamented, not only with external decorations, but with the statues and pictures of the most distinguished astronomers, and with inscriptions and poems in their honour.

Having at length completed his observatory, and furnished it with instruments of the finest possible description, Tycho devoted himself to the examination of the stars; and during the twenty years which he passed at Huen, he made vast additions to astronomical knowledge, noticing every phenomenon that appeared in the heavens with great accuracy, and carrying on a regular series of observations for determining the places of the fixed stars, and for improving the tables of the sun, moon, and planets. In order to advance the interests of the science, he took under his roof several pupils, whom he instructed; some of whom were sent by the king, and maintained at his expense, while others, who voluntarily offered themselves, were liberally admitted by the generous astronomer.

Having expended nearly £20,000 of his own money in his outlay at Uraniberg, his income was so much reduced that the king settled on him a pension of 1000 crowns per annum, and gave him, in addition, a canonry of Roskild, which was worth about twice that amount. The career of the great astronomer was now one of rare prosperity. When scarcely thirty years of age, he found himself established by the royal favour in the most splendid observatory Europe had ever possessed; he was happy in his domestic relations; had an extended reputation among the wisest of his contemporaries; and was at liberty to pursue the science he devotedly loved, and upon which his heart had always been set. Although almost entirely absorbed in his favourite pursuits, he did not act the part of a recluse or a misanthrope; on the contrary, he kept open house, and received with generous hospitality the crowds of inquirers, nobles, and princes, who came to visit him in the splendid temple he had consecrated to science.

Among other persons of distinction who found their way to Uraniberg was our James VI. of Scotland, who passed a week there in the year 1590, attended by a large suite of nobility. On his departure, the monarch presented his host with a

TYCHO AND THE SCOTTISH SOVEREIGN.

munificent donation, granted him his royal license to publish his works in England, and passed a high eulogium on his abilities and learning.

Some interesting particulars have been preserved relative to the personal appearance and manners of Tycho, which may assist us in forming an idea of the home life and ways of the man. He was rather above the middle size, of florid complexion, with reddish-yellow hair, and latterly became slightly corpulent. Naturally sanguine and hasty in temperament, he was very plain-spoken, and often irritable in temper; but in his domestic circle (where only a man is rightly appreciated as to disposition) he appears to have secured the affectionate regard of all. Both his pupils and scientific friends were greatly attached to him, and some of the former remained inmates of his house for more than twenty years. Proudly independent in feeling, and conscious of elevated motives, he could ill brook the assumption and impertinence of certain personages high in office, with whom he came in contact; and consequently he incurred the dislike of some, who waited their opportunity to do him an ill turn. Like not a few men of genius, he possessed a turn for satire, which he occasionally indulged unwisely. As he was by no means willing to take as much as he gave, this weakness rendered him liable to frequent mortifications. He was given, too, to the indulgence of practical jokes; but his kindly feeling preserved him from intentionally inflicting pain.

The same disposition of mind which made Tycho an astrologer and an alchemist, inspired him with a singular love of the marvellous. Strange as it may seem, we learn that he delighted in mystifying and astonishing his visitors with a variety of contrivances calculated to deceive and puzzle. For instance, he constructed several automata, with the movements of which he amazed the rustics and peasants, who in their simplicity believed them to be spirits. He was fond of being consulted as a fortune-teller, and encouraged the idea that his acquaintance with the heavenly bodies enabled him to predict events. By means of invisible bells, which communicated with every part of the establishment, he used unexpectedly to summon his pupils and attendants, who appeared, as though by magic, when he muttered their names.

One of his most extraordinary fancies was to keep an idiot, named Zep, who sat at his feet during meal times, and whom he fed with his own hand. This unfortunate being occasionally uttered incoherent expressions, which his master carefully noted, from a persuasion that he was capable, in certain states, of foretelling coming events. Various statements in the letters of Tycho's correspondents refer to these supposed predictions; and it is a proof of the superstition of the age, that these learned men repeated them as worthy of credence.

One of the extravagant pretensions of the alchemists was that of forming a universal medicine; and Tycho was a dabbler in physic, liked to be consulted, gave his medicines and advice gratis, and invented an elixir which he called an infallible cure for epidemic disorders—of which celebrated medicine he gave the recipe to the Emperor Rodolph, begging him to preserve it secret, and to keep the remedy for himself alone!

These foibles show that even spirits of a nobler mould are not exempt from human ignorance and frailty. It is at the same time worthy of remark, and a curious fact, that though Tycho declared he had devoted as much labour and expense to the study of alchemy as to that of astronomy, he never published any account of his experiments, nor did he leave among his writings any trace of them. There is reason to believe that in his latter days he renounced these fallacies, and that his mind was entirely emancipated from the superstitions of astrology.

Unhappily for the interests of Danish science, Frederic II. died in the year 1588, at the age of fifty-four. His son and successor, Christian IV., was but eleven years old when this event occurred. When he had attained the age of fourteen, he expressed a desire to visit Uraniberg, and showed great curiosity in examining the various treasures of the place. Among other things, he particularly admired a brass globe, which was moved by means of internal clock-work. Tycho made him a present of this curious machine, and received in return a gold chain and his majesty's picture, with assurances of his unalterable favour and protection.

Notwithstanding these fair promises, it appears that the enemies of the great astronomer were already plotting mischief, and their machinations were not so secret but that Tycho had some idea of them. Writing to his friend the Landgrave of Hesse, early in 1591, he threw out some hints of the anxieties that agitated his mind; and in a touching manner expressed a hope, that if he should be involved in the troubles and tumults of life, either by his own destiny or by evil counsels, he might be able, by the blessing of God, to extricate himself by the strength of his mind and the integrity of his life. He comforted himself with the idea that every soil was the country of a great man, and that wherever he went, the firmament would still be overhead; and he distinctly said at the close of the letter, that he had thought of transferring his residence elsewhere, as some of the king's counsellors had already begun to calumniate his studies, and to grudge him his pension from the treasury.

Whatever the causes of this ill-will on the part of the advisers of Christian IV., the results were truly lamentable. Tycho was deprived of his canonry, his estate in Norway, and his pension; and as he was no longer able to bear the expenses of his establishment at Huen, he resolved to remove thence. In the first instance, he took a house in Copenhagen; but his opponents behaved in so hostile a manner, that he determined no longer to remain in an ungrateful country. He carried out to the full this decision, and removed from Huen everything that was moveable. Having packed up all his instruments, crucibles, and books, he hired a ship, on board which he embarked with his wife, five sons and four daughters, his men and women servants, and many of his pupils and assistants. Crossing the Baltic, this precious freight arrived safely at Rostock, where for a while the exiles found a resting-place, and afterwards removed to Wandsberg, near Hamburg, at the invitation of Count Rantzau.

Tycho was not long without a patron and a permanent residence. At the close of 1598 he received a pressing invitation from the Emperor Rodolph II., promising him every assistance for the prosecution of his scientific studies if he would remove with all his apparatus to the imperial dominions. Accordingly in the following spring he proceeded to Prague, where he was most cordially welcomed by the emperor, who settled upon him a handsome pension, and offered him the choice of various residences as the site of his observatory. He gave the preference to Benach, a beautiful place, situated five miles from the capital, and called the Venice of Bohemia. In Prague he found a numerous circle of friends and admiring associates, and if external circumstances could have availed to remove the sorrows and regrets of the past, he might have been content and happy. But the death blow had been struck when he quitted his beloved home. Notwithstanding the liberality of the emperor, and the kindness of his friends and pupils—among the latter of whom was the illustrious Kepler—he felt himself a stranger and an outcast. He had hitherto enjoyed excellent health, but he now began to feel symptoms of complaints that announced approaching dissolution, though for a time he carefully concealed them. His constitution was so much weakened, and his nerves so greatly shaken, that the most trifling incidents overcame him with alarm. This excited state of mind was the forerunner of a fatal disorder, with which he was attacked in the autumn of 1601. A violent access of the malady so greatly reduced him, that, after a few days' distressing suffering, he expired on the 24th October, in the 55th year of his age.

The account given of his last hours is very impressive. During the intervals of delirium he was heard frequently to utter the words, "Ne frustra vixisse videor;" a touching expression of the yearnings of his soul: "Let me not have lived in vain," exclaimed the dying enthusiast. The aspiration is one breathed by all kindred souls, and bespeaks the *mens divina*. Be of good cheer, thou earnest spirit! Not in vain hast thou struggled and laboured, and endured sacrifice and reproach in the pursuit of thine object. Verily thou hast thy reward, in the approbation of Him who gave thee talents, and furnished thee with the means thou didst turn to good account;

in the admiration of all congenial natures, and in the gratitude of succeeding generations, who have reaped the benefit of those researches which, it is acknowledged, formed the first great step of the moderns in astronomy.

Not many hours before his decease, consciousness being fully restored, Tycho perceiving his condition, recommended to his family devout resignation to the divine will, expressed a fervent desire that his labours should redound to the glory of his Maker, uttered prayers and sang hymns, then bade farewell to his pupils, exhorting them not to abandon their studies, and requesting Kepler to complete a work upon which they had been employed together. And thus " amidst prayers, exhortations, and friendly converse, he expired so peaceably that he was neither heard nor seen by any of those present to breathe his last."

Sir David Brewster, after reviewing the history and the works of Tycho Brahe, says, "As a practical astronomer he has not been surpassed by any observer of ancient or of modern times. The splendour and number of his instruments, the ingenuity which he exhibited in inventing new ones, and improving and adding to those which were formerly known, and his skill and assiduity as an observer, have given a character to his labours and a value to his observations which will be appreciated to the latest posterity."

Tom Britton,

THE MUSICAL SMALL-COAL MAN.

THE musical cries of the London street-vendors were formerly much in repute, and, at one time, the public were frequently amused at the theatres by actors who mimicked them with great skill. Some curious anecdotes with reference to this subject are related in Smith's "Life of Nollekens." He mentions, in particular, two very singular cries; the first of them was used by an itinerant dealer in corks, sometimes called "Old Corks," who rode upon an ass, and carried his wares in panniers on each side of him. He sat with much dignity, and wore upon his head a velvet cap; and his attractive cry, which was partly spoken and partly sung, but all in metre, was something like the following fragment:—

Spoken.—" Corks for sack, I have at my back;
Sung.—All handy, all handy; some for wine and some for brandy.
Spoken.—Corks for gin, very thin;
Corks for rum, as big as my thumb;
Corks for ale, long and pale;
Sung.—They're all handy, all handy; some for wine and some for brandy.

The other cry, which was much more musical,

was that of two persons, father and son, who sold lines. The father, in a strong, clear tenor, would begin the strain in the major key, and when he had finished, his son, who followed at a short distance behind him, in a shrill falsetto, would repeat it in the minor, and their call consisted of the following words:—

> "Buy a white-line, or a jack-line,
> Or a clock-line, or a hair-line,
> Or a line for your clothes here."

The music of several of these cries was noted down by persons curious in these matters, and Smith relates that in a copy of Hawkins's "History of Music," in the British Museum, is the following MS. note respecting the famous Tom Britton, the musical small-coal man :—"The goodness of his ear directed him to the use of the most perfect of all musical intervals, the diapason or octave."

Probably most of our readers are hardly acquainted with the use or even the name of small coal. Dr. Johnson defines it: "Small coal, little wood coals, used to light fires," and illustrates the word from the *Spectator*, and Gay :—

> "A small-coal man, by waking one of these distressed gentlemen, saved him from ten years' imprisonment."—*Spectator*.

> "When small-coal murmurs in the hoarser throat,
> From smutty dangers guard thy threatened coat."
> *Gay's Trivia.*

Some century ago small-coal was daily cried about the streets, and of general use, in the capital at least, in kindling fires. Of Thomas Britton, who followed this humble profession, Mr. Walpole in his "Anecdotes" says, that "Woolaston the painter, who was a good performer on the violin and flute, had played at the concert held at the house of that extraordinary person, Thomas Britton, the small-coal man, whose picture he twice drew, one of which portraits was purchased by Sir Hans Sloane, and is now in the British Museum; there is a mezzotinto from it. This man, who made such a noise in his time, considering his low station and trade, was a collector of all sorts of curiosities, particularly drawings, prints, books, MSS. on uncommon subjects, as mystic divinity, the philosopher's stone, judicial astrology, and magic, and musical instruments both in and out of vogue. Various were the opinions concerning him; some thought his musical assembly only a cover for seditious meetings; others, for magical purposes. He was taken for an atheist, a Presbyterian, a Jesuit. But Woolaston the painter, and the son of a gentleman, who had likewise been a member of his club, averred it as their opinions that Britton was a simple, honest man, who only meant to amuse himself. The subscription was but ten shillings a year; Britton found the instruments, and they had coffee at a penny a dish. Sir Hans Sloane bought many of his books and MSS., now in the Museum, when they were sold by auction at Tom's coffee house, near Ludgate."

This account is perfectly in accordance with the

manner in which Britton was spoken of by many of his contemporaries. So late as the middle of the last century, mezzotint prints of him were in all the print-shops, particularly an excellent one by Smith, under which were these verses, written by Hughes, who himself frequently performed on the violin at the concerts of this ingenious small-coal man:—

> "Though mean thy rank, yet in thy humble cell
> Did gentle peace and arts, unpurchased, dwell ;
> Well pleased Apollo thither led his train
> And music warbled in her sweetest strain.
> Cyllenius so, as fables tell, and Jove
> Came willing guests to poor Philemon's grove.
> Let useless pomp behold, and blush to find
> So low a station, such a liberal mind."

In most of the prints he was represented with his sack of small-coal on his shoulder, and his measure of retail in his hand.

Britton was a great favourite with Hearne, the celebrated antiquary, whom he much resembled in his fondness for old things, and who has given a long account of him in one of his works, wherein he informs us that Britton was born at or near Higham Ferrers, in Northamptonshire, from which place he went to London, where he bound himself apprentice to a small-coal man. After he had served his full term of seven years, his master gave him a sum of money not to set up. Upon this Tom returned into Northamptonshire and spent his money, after which he went back to the metropolis and set up a small-coal trade, though his master was still living, taking a stable in Clerkenwell, which he turned into a house. This dishonourable action, which truth compels us to relate, was the only one of the kind with which he was ever chargeable.

Some time after he had been settled in business thus, he became acquainted with Dr. Garaniere, his neighbour, an eminent chemist, who admitted him into his laboratory, where, by the doctor's assistance and his own acuteness of observation, he soon became a notable chemist, and himself contrived and built a moving laboratory, in which, if Hearne may be credited, " he performed with little expense and trouble such things as had never been done before."

Beside his great skill in chemistry, he became a practical, and, as was thought, a theoretical musician. It is related that he was very fond of music, and that he was able to perform on the vial da gamba, at his own concerts, which he at first established gratis in his miserable house, which was an old, mean building, the ground floor of which was a repository for his small coal ; over this was his concert room, long, low, and narrow, to which there was no ascent but by a pair of stairs outside, so perpendicular and narrow as scarcely to be mounted without crawling.

Hearne states him to have been a very diligent collector of old books of all kinds, which, in his courses through the town, crying his small-coal, he had a good opportunity of finding at stalls, where he used to stop, and select for purchase whatever was ancient,

BRITTON AT A BOOK-STALL.

particularly on his two favourite subjects of Chemistry and Music. Of the former, it has been suggested that he had picked up books on the Rosicrucian mysteries; and it is not impossible but that he wasted some of his small-coals in the great secrets of alchemy and the transmutation of metals.

Of the latter, he procured all the elementary books

in English, which were then extant, and, besides his vast collection of printed music, the catalogue of which fills eight pages in quarto of Sir J. Hawkins's History of Music, he seems to have been such an indefatigable copyist, that he is said to have transcribed with his own hands, very neatly and accurately, a collection of music, which sold, after his decease, for nearly £100.

Britton's reputation was so great, that Steele, speaking, in the *Guardian*, of a variety of original and odd characters, added: "We have now a small-coal man, who, beginning with two plain notes, which constituted his daily cry, has made himself master of the whole compass of the gammut, and has frequent concerts of music at his own house, for the entertainment of himself and friends." But it appears, the assertion of Sir John Hawkins that Britton was the first who had a meeting that corresponded with the idea of a concert, is not correct; since, in Charles II.'s time, the Banisters, father and son, had concerts—first at taverns and public-houses, and afterwards at York Buildings.

It should seem that, at the commencement of the last century, a passion prevailed among several persons of distinction for collecting old books and MSS.; and we are told, it was their Saturday's amusement, during winter, to ramble through various quarters of the town in pursuit of these treasures. The Earls of Pembroke, Sunderland, and Winchelsea, and the Duke of Devonshire, were of this party, and Mr. Bagford, and other collectors, assisted them in their researches. Britton appears to have been employed by these gentlemen; and being a very modest, decent, and unpresuming man, he was a sharer in their conversation, when they met after their morning's walk at a bookseller's shop in Ave Maria Lane. Britton used to pitch his coal sack on a bulk at the door, and, dressed in his blue frock, to step in and spend an hour with the company. But it was not by a few literary lords alone that his acquaintance was cultivated. His humble roof was frequented by assemblies of the fair and gay; and his fondness for music caused him to be known by many professors and dilettanti, who formed themselves into a club at his house, where capital pieces were played by some of the first professional artists and other practitioners; and here Dubourg, the eminent violinist, when a child, played, standing upon a joint-stool, the first solo he ever executed in public.

The circumstances of Britton's death were as extraordinary as those of his life, if the accounts given by Dr. Aikin in his biography be correct. A ventriloquist was introduced to his company by an acquaintance who was fond of those mischievous tricks commonly called "practical jokes." This fellow, in a voice which apparently came from a vast distance, announced to poor Britton his approaching end, and bade him prepare for it, by repeating the

Lord's Prayer, on his knees. The credulous dupe, whose mystical and magical books had probably weakened his reasoning powers, obeyed the injunction, and, returning home, took to his bed, and actually died in a few days. This was in September 1714. He was buried, with a very respectful attendance, in Clerkenwell churchyard.

Giobanni Battista Belzoni.

CERTAINLY one of the most enterprising and sagacious of modern explorers, Belzoni, was a man of no common mould; and his history can hardly fail to interest the readers of these sketches.

He was born at Padua, in 1778, but his family came originally from Rome, as he himself says in the preface to his work on Egypt. His father, who was a barber by trade, was poor and had a numerous family. Giovanni seems early to have shown a propensity for wandering. When thirteen years old, he set out with a younger brother for an excursion, and having met with a chance conveyance, was taken as far as Ferrara. Finding himself actually on his travels, the lad, whose anxiety was to see Rome, of which he had heard his parents often talk, determined, if possible, to reach that wonderful city; and he actually contrived to get to the Apennines, where, however, he was compelled to abandon his project, by the complaints and exhaustion of Antonio, his little brother. Sorrowfully retracing his steps to

Padua, the young enthusiast settled, however unwillingly, to his father's trade for a while. Not, however, for long: at the end of three years he was again on his way to the Eternal City, and this time he was without a companion. He has casually mentioned that he lived several years in Rome, and that he learned there the science of hydraulics; but he has given no information as to the way in which he gained a living, merely saying—"My family supplied me occasionally with remittances; but as they were not rich, I did not choose to be a burden to them, and contrived to live on my own industry, and a little knowledge I had acquired in various branches."

Apparently he was driven to great shifts; for he had determined on becoming a monk—a vocation for which he certainly could not have felt any natural disposition—when the arrival of the French armies in Italy, in 1800, wrought an entire change in his fortunes. He hastened to abandon his monastic projects, and quitting Rome, wandered about from city to city in different parts of Europe, "suffering," as he says, "many vicissitudes." He remained for a year in Holland, and, in 1803, visited England, where he continued about nine years. Shortly after his arrival in this country he married an Englishwoman, to whom he seems to have been faithfully and warmly attached; and from that time she was the constant attendant upon and the sharer of all his wanderings and varying fortunes. Belzoni was in person of a surprising size and of athletic proportions. He was nearly six feet eight inches in height, very strong, and of extraordinary muscular powers, which were of great service to him throughout his career. For a considerable time after he was in England, he gained a maintenance by perambulating the country performing feats of agility and strength, exhibiting hydraulic experiments, musical glasses, and phantasmagoria. He was afterwards engaged for some time at Astley's amphitheatre; and in various ways he managed to live, until, in 1812, he sailed with his wife for Lisbon, where he soon made an engagement with the director of the San Carlos theatre. There he appeared, during Lent, in the character of Samson, with great success, for a whole season, and afterwards at Madrid, where he attracted much attention by his performances before the king and the court.

Having thus succeeded in procuring the necessary funds, Belzoni proceeded to Malta, where he fell in with Ishmael Gibraltar, the agent of the Pasha, the renowned Mahomet Ali, who at that time governed Egypt. To this man he talked of his skill in hydraulics, and, by his recommendation, was induced to go to Alexandria, in the hope of obtaining employment in the service of the Egyptian ruler.

Incredible as it may seem, upon this slender hope he ventured to transport himself, with his wife, and a little Irish lad, named Curtain, whom he had engaged as his servant, into a strange land, amidst an unknown race, of whose language he was ignorant, and without a friend on whom he could rely for assistance. Nothing could be more discouraging than his first adventures in the land of the Pharaohs. He had no sooner reached the harbour of Alexandria than he was greeted with the fearful tidings that the plague was in the city, and for several days he was compelled to remain a close prisoner. At length he proceeded to Cairo, where he was to be presented to the Pasha; but this interview was delayed for some time by a savage attack made upon him, when passing through the narrow streets, by a soldier, who struck him so violent a blow on the leg, that it was thirty days before he could stand. This brutality, for which he could obtain no redress, was wholly unprovoked, merely occasioned by the impatience of the wretch, who wanted to pass more quickly than Belzoni's movements permitted.

When he had sufficiently recovered, he presented himself to Ali Pasha, who immediately engaged him to make a machine for watering his seraglio gardens. Full of hope that he was now on the way to prosperity, he commenced his operations with great alacrity. In his travels there is a very pleasing account of his first impressions at sight of the glorious monuments of antiquity, which were so soon to engage all his skill and enterprise. He says—"Though my object at this time was not antiquities, I could not restrain myself from going to see the wonder of the world, the Pyramids. I took care to ascend the first pyramid early enough in the morning to see the rising of the sun, and was on the top of it long before the dawn of day. The scene here is majestic and grand, far beyond description: a mist over the plains of Egypt formed a veil, which ascended and vanished gradually as the sun rose, and unveiled to the view the beautiful land, once the site of Memphis. The distant view of the smaller pyramids on the south marked the extension of that vast capital, while the solemn, endless spectacle of the desert on the west inspired reverence for the all-powerful Creator. The fertile lands on the north, with the serpentine course of the Nile, which flows magnificently through the centre of the sacred valley, and the thick groves of palm trees, with the rich appearance of Cairo and its numerous minarets, at the foot of the Mokatam mountain on the east, all together formed a scene of which very imperfect ideas can be given by the most elaborate description. I returned thence to Cairo, with the satisfaction of having seen a wonder which I had long desired, but never supposed I should have the happiness, to behold."

Belzoni relates that he succeeded completely, to the Pasha's satisfaction, in the construction of his machine; but the undertaking eventually failed through the insurmountable prejudices and obstacles he had to encounter in the course of his proceedings. At the first trial made of it an accident occurred, which was regarded by the bystanders as a bad omen, and the Turkish assistants refused to work it. In consequence of this mischance, Belzoni was dismissed from his employment, and became reduced to a state of want, bordering on destitution. Under these circumstances, he determined to try his fortune in search of antiquities—an occupation to which several of his countrymen had given themselves, though without much result; but his great difficulty was the want of the necessary funds. Just at this crisis accident introduced him to the notice of Messrs. Burckhardt and Salt, the latter of whom was then the English consul in Egypt, and had just arrived in Cairo. These gentlemen were exceedingly desirous to secure the removal of the colossal head, generally called that of the younger Memnon, from Thebes to Alexandria. Being much struck by the manly appearance and remarkably engaging manners of Belzoni, they determined to employ him in the work, at their joint expense, and he very gladly acceded to their proposal.

The success which crowned his efforts in the accomplishment of this arduous undertaking, was the foundation of his future prosperity. It afforded him the means of distinguishing himself, and he became, on account of his discoveries, the object of European admiration.

The difficulty attendant upon such an enterprise no one will question who has ever viewed that magnificent specimen of Egyptian art in the British Museum. To accomplish its transit it was necessary, after dragging it down upwards of a mile to the water side, to place it on board a small boat, to convey it thence to Rosetta, and afterwards to land and lodge it in a magazine at Alexandria; all which was most surprisingly effected with the assistance solely of the native peasantry, and such simple machinery as Belzoni was able to get made under his directions at Cairo. He thus describes his first sight of the treasure,—" As I entered the ruins my first thought was to examine the colossal bust I had to take away. I found it near the remains of its body and chair, with its face upwards, and *apparently smiling on me at the thought of being taken to England.*" This imaginative trait gives us a clue to the genuine nature of the man, who could thus, in the face of obstacles sufficient to daunt the most stout-hearted, find, if not "*Sermons* in stones," a mute eloquence which sufficed to prompt him to successful effort. Belzoni had now found his proper sphere, and henceforward he devoted himself entirely to the work of exploring the marvels of this wondrous land, and, as his employer states, " his great talents and uncommon genius for mechanics enabled him, with singular success, both at Thebes and other places, to discover objects of the rarest value which had long baffled

BELZONI'S FIRST SIGHT OF THE YOUNGER MEMNON.

the researches of the learned; and with trifling means to remove colossal fragments which appear, by their own declaration, to have defied the efforts of the able engineers who accompanied the French army." His next undertaking was to proceed beyond the second cataract, with the purpose of opening the magnificent temple at Ipsamboul. This was a work of great difficulty and no inconsiderable risk, and presented obstacles which probably nothing but the personal strength and persevering spirit of Belzoni could have enable him to overcome. Every obstruction, however, seemed destined to fall before the sagacity and gigantic efforts of this extraordinary man. The natives whom he had hired to assist him, after working a few days, refused to go on, and finally left the party to its own resources. Thus deserted, Belzoni, with the assisttance of Mr. Beechy, who had accompanied him, determined to persist in the apparently hopeless labour. To add to their difficulties the sheik of the place forbad the natives to supply them with provisions, and they had nothing left in their boat but a bag of millet, and on this and the Nile water they managed to support themselves during one and twenty days of the severest labour, at the end of which their most sanguine expectations were realized by uncovering and penetrating into the interior of the temple.

Some idea of this herculean task may be formed when we are told that two-thirds of this extensive temple were completely buried in the sand, and in some places to the height of fifty feet, the whole of which enormous mass had to be removed before the structure could be approached!

The truly surprising exertions of Belzoni induced Mr. Salt to employ him again in the following year; and in the month of Feburary 1817, he, with Mr. Beechy, left Cairo to prosecute further their researches. During the following ten months in which Belzoni remained in the employ of the English Consul, he succeeded in completely uncovering the front of the temple at Ipsamboul, opened six tombs in the valley of Biban el Moluck (the tombs of the kings), found in one of them the celebrated alabaster sarcophagus, and at Thebes discovered a colossal head of Horus, of fine granite, and the finest workmanship, and many other minor remains.

Of the tomb above mentioned, Mr. Salt says:—"It consists of a long suite of passages and chambers, covered with sculptures and paintings in the most perfect state of preservation, the tints of which are so resplendent that it was found scarcely possible to imitate them with the best water colours made in England; and which, in fact, are executed in a way that would make them, I conceive, retain their lustre even by the side of a Venetian picture."

Belzoni's own account of his emotions at first examining Karnak is very striking. "In a distant view of these superb ruins," he says, "nothing can be seen but the towering porpylœa, high portals and obelisks, which rise above the groups of lofty palm trees, and even from afar announce magnificence. On approaching the avenue of sphinxes which leads to the great temple, the visitor is inspired with devotion and piety. Still further on was the magnificent temple dedicated to the great God of the creation. It was the first time I entered it alone—the sun was rising, and the long shades from the various groups of columns extended over the ruins, intermixed with the rays of light striking on these masses in various directions, forming such delightful views as baffle all description. My mind was impressed with ideas of such solemnity, that for some time I was unconscious whether I was on terrestrial ground. I found myself lost in a mass of colossal objects. How can I describe my sensations at that moment! I seemed alone in the midst of all that is most sacred in the world; a forest of enormous columns, adorned all round with beautiful figures and various ornaments, from the top to the bottom; the graceful shape of the lotus, which forms their capitals; the gates, walls, pedestals, and architraves, also adorned in every part with symbolical figures representing battles, processions, triumphs, feasts, sacrifices, and offerings, all relating, doubtless, to the ancient history of the country; the sanctuary, formed wholly of red granite; its high portals seen at a distance from the openings to this vast labyrinth of edifices; altogether such an effect was produced on my soul as to cause me to forget entirely the trifles and follies of life. I was happy for a whole day, which fled like a flash of lightning, but the obscurity of the night caused me to stumble over one large block of stone, and to break my nose against another, and thus dissolving the enchantment, brought me to my senses again. It was quite late when I returned to Luxor, to the hut of an Arab, who gave me part of his chamber and a mat, which afforded me an excellent bed."

He thus describes his discovery of the principal tomb at Biban el Moluck:—"On the 16th October, I pointed out the fortunate spot which has paid me for all the trouble I took in my researches. I may call this a fortunate day; one of the best perhaps in my life. I do not mean to say that fortune has made me rich—but she has given me that satisfaction, that extreme pleasure which wealth cannot purchase; the pleasure of discovering what had been long sought in vain, and of presenting to the world a new and perfect monument of Egyptian antiquity."

He goes on to relate the way in which he discovered the locality of the tomb, and how with great labour and the most ingenious contrivance, he succeeded in penetrating this rock-cut ancient abode of the dead. "At length," he says, "we reached the central saloon, where we found a sarcophagus of the finest oriental alabaster, nine feet five inches long, and three feet seven inches wide. Its thickness is only two inches, and it is transparent when a light is placed in the inside of it. It is minutely sculptured within and without with several hundred figures, which do not exceed two inches in height, and

A GORGEOUS INTERIOR. 111

BELZONI IN THE GRAND TOMB AT THEBES.

represent, as I suppose, the whole of the funeral procession and ceremonies relative to the deceased, united with several emblems, &c. The cover was not there; it had been taken out and broken into several pieces, which we found in digging before the first entrance.

Belzoni made drawings of the various chambers, took impressions in wax of the figures and hieroglyphics, carefully noting the various colours, and thus constructed a perfect facsimile of this magnificent tomb, which was afterwards exhibited in London and Paris. This work occupied him more than twelve months.

On returning to Cairo from this grand discovery, he immediately engaged in a new research, which led, perhaps, to a still more important discovery. He determined to make an attempt to penetrate one of the pyramids, and at length succeeded in his undertaking. It had long been considered an object of so hopeless a nature that it is difficult to conceive how any one could be found sanguine enough to make the attempt. Nothing could present a more hopeless prospect on outward examination, than the point where he came upon the true entrance; nevertheless, the direct manner in which he dug down upon the door afforded the most incontestible proof that he did not work by chance. Of the labour as well as the skill exerted no one can form an adequate idea. The whole of this operation was effected too, entirely at his own risk and expense. In the centre of the pyramid of Cephrenes (as it was called), he found a sarcophagus, containing the bones of a bull; a discovery which has been considered to prove that these immense structures were built by the ancient Egyptians as sepulchres for their brute deities.

The opening of this pyramid was nearly the last, as it was perhaps the greatest, of Belzoni's undertakings, and the sagacity and perseverance he displayed on the occasion greatly added to his former reputation.

In the autumn of 1818, he again left Cairo and went to Esne, from whence he struck across the desert to the shores of the Red Sea. He there discovered the ruins of the ancient town of Berenice, and visited also the emerald mines of Mount Zabarah. In the following year he journeyed to Lake Mœris, and from thence to the smaller Oasis, which no European had previously visited.

At length, in September 1819, Belzoni quitted Egypt after a residence of five years in that country. He first returned to his native land, and revisited his birthplace, which he had left twenty years before, a needy youth, obscurely born, and with the slenderest means of support. How changed were now his circumstances! He had a name renowned through every country of Europe, and the glory of his achievements made him the pride of his fellow-citizens. On this occasion he presented to the town of Padua two lion-headed granite statues, which were placed, by order of the magistrates, on the Palace of Justice, and a medal engraved by Manfredini, was struck in honour of the illustrious traveller, bearing his name, and recording his deeds.

From Italy he hastened to England, which had reaped so valuable a harvest from his labours, and where he was received with the warmest expressions of admiration and welcome. During several months he occupied himself in preparing an account of his Travels and Discoveries for the press, which appeared at the close of 1820, in a quarto volume, accompanied by a folio one of plates. This work excited the greatest interest, and passed through three editions. It was translated into French and Italian. Its author then visited the continent, and passed successively into France, Russia, Sweden, and Denmark; after which he returned to England, and, doubtless prompted by the spirit of adventure within him, determined upon undertaking the perilous attempt —in which so many enterprising men had already perished—of penetrating into the interior of Africa. His plan was to endeavour, in the first instance, to reach Timbuctoo, and thence direct his course eastward towards Sennaar, and then to return through Nubia and Egypt.

Before leaving England he visited different parts of England, and among other places, Norwich, where he was introduced to Mr. Brightwell, whose acquaintance with Natural History was the occasion of his interview with the celebrated traveller. Belzoni left behind him a slight and delicate memorial of this visit in a faint sketch he drew on the blank page of a copy of Latreille's "Memoirs." It represents a rude figure of a winged insect, and beneath it Mr. Brightwell has written,—"This figure was drawn by Belzoni, the Egyptian traveller, as a hieroglyphic of what he thought a locust, commonly sculptured upon obelisks, &c., and which M. Latreille thinks meant for a sphix. (This occurs in the chapter on the Sacred Insects of Egypt). Belzoni said he had never seen any real scarabœi done up with the mummies; only the sculptured figures."

He took his final leave of England towards the close of 1822, and sailed for Gibraltar, whence—accompanied by his wife—he proceeded to Tangier, and then to the city of Fez, where, being favourably received by the emperor of Morocco, he hoped to accomplish his purpose of reaching Tafilelt, and joining the caravan which assembles there to cross the Desert of Soudan.

Unhappily, his expectations were disappointed and his plans frustrated by the jealousies of the traders, who succeeded in thwarting all his efforts. After five months thus vainly spent, he was compelled to relinquish this route, and repairing to Mogadore, he embarked for Cape Coast, whence he proceeded to the Bight of Benin, with the hope of reaching the Niger. He was landed at Benin by Captain Filmore of the *Owen Glendower* frigate, who showed him every attention in his power, and discharged from his crew a negro, who was a native of Houssa, and who undertook to accompany Belzoni thither. In a letter from this gentleman are given a few particulars relative to the last days of our traveller's life. It is dated from British Accra, January 7, 1824:—"On the night of the 24th November, Mr. Belzoni left us with Mr. Houtson for Gato. On parting with us he seemed a little agitated, particularly when the crew, to each of whom he had made a present, gave him three loud cheers on leaving the vessel. 'God bless you, my fine fellows, and send you a happy sight of your country and friends!' was his answer. On the 3d December, I received a letter from Mr. Houtson, requesting me to go to Benin as Mr. Belzoni was dangerously ill. I was prevented going by a severe fever which was then upon me. On the 5th I got another letter, giving the particulars of his end, and one from himself, almost illegible, dated December 2, requesting me to assist in the disposal of his effects, and to remit the proceeds to his agents in London, together with a beautiful amethyst ring he wore, which he seemed particularly anxious should be delivered to his wife, with the assurance he died in the fullest affection for her, as he found himself too weak to write his last wishes and adieus."

At the time of Belzoni's death, everything had been arranged with the King of Benin for his departure; he passed for a native of the interior, who had gone to England when a youth, and was now returning to his country. He wore his Moorish dress, and his beard was nearly a foot in length. By a few presents, well applied, he had succeeded in removing the obstacles put in his way by the authorities, and all seemed to promise fair for his success. But the hand of death was upon him, and the deadly climate had already stricken the fatal blow. Perceiving that his malady was severe, he begged to be taken back to the coast, but was unable to reach it, and expired at Gato on the 3d December, 1823. He was buried the day following his decease, and a board with the following inscription, was placed over his grave:—

"HERE LIE THE REMAINS OF G. BELZONI,
WHO WAS ATTACKED WITH DYSENTERY AT BENIN,
(ON HIS WAY TO HOUSSA AND TIMBUCTOO)
AND DIED AT THIS PLACE, DEC. 3, 1823."

Such was the melancholy end of Belzoni, a man whose history speaks for itself, and shows what natural shrewdness, perseverance, and indomitable energy may effect. Had chance afforded him the opportunity of exerting his talents in the pursuit of the science of mechanics, he would probably have greatly excelled in that direction. Those who knew him said he was frank and kind-hearted, but too sensitive to any supposed injuries or slights, in consequence of which he was often in collision with those around him. Whatever his real or imaginary faults, he had many excellent qualities, and deserves to be ever remembered as the intrepid pioneer of Egyptian research and discovery.

Dr. Alexander Murray.

THIS great linguist was an eminent example of what the force of native talent will sometimes accomplish where education has been almost wholly withheld. His early history is a very interesting one, and is given by himself in a short autobiography prefixed to his posthumous work, "The History of European Languages." He was born at Dunkitterick, in the shire of Kirkcudbright, on the 22d October, 1775. His father, who was at the time of his birth, nearly seventy years old, had a large family of sons, all of whom he had brought up to his own calling, which was that of a shepherd, as his father's had been before him. His humble cottage was in a dark and lonely glen, buried among hills, which were traversed by no strangers but smugglers, and all his property consisted of four muirland cows, and some two or three scores of sheep. The old man, as described by his son, was a fine character:—" He had been taught to read English in a good style for his time. He wrote not badly, but exactly like the old men of the seventeenth century. He had a considerable share of acuteness, or natural sagacity, a quality possessed by most of his clan. His temper was rather irritable, but not passionate. His moral character was habitually good; and I knew, from his way of talking in private about thefts and rogueries of other persons, that he actually detested these vices. He was very religious in private; but in company he was merry, fond of old stories, and of singing. My brother, James, his youngest son by the first marriage, died of a fever in 1781, or 1782. His death, which happened at some distance from home, was reported to my father early on a Sunday morning, and I, then a child, could not conceive why my father wept and prayed all that day."

Good, tender-hearted old man! this touching incident gives us a glimpse into his heart, and makes us feel how, in "the far nooks of this wide-peopled earth," there are to be found some of the truest and the best of our kind. His son tells us he enjoyed hale good health, till shortly before his death, which occurred at the patriarchal age of ninety-one.

From him Alexander received his first lessons in reading. "Some time in autumn 1781, he bought a catechism for me, and began to teach me the alphabet. As it was too good a book for me to handle at all times, it was generally locked up, and he, throughout the winter, drew the figures of the letters to me in his *written* hand on the board of an

MURRAY'S FIRST LESSON.

old *wool-card* with the black end of an extinguished heather stem or root, snatched from the fire. I soon learned all the alphabet in this form, and became writer as well as reader. I wrought with the *board* and *brand* continually. Then the catechism was presented; and in a month or two I could read the easier parts of it. I daily amused myself with copying, as above, the *printed* letters. In May, 1782, he gave me a small psalm book, for which I totally abandoned the catechism, which I did not like, and which I tore into two pieces and concealed in a hole of a dike. I soon got many psalms by memory, and longed for a new book. Here difficulties arose. The Bible, used every night in the family, I was not permitted to open or touch. The rest of the books were put up in chests. I at length got a New Testament, and read the historical parts with great curiosity and ardour. But I longed to read the Bible, which seemed to me a much more pleasant book, and I actually went to where I knew an old loose-leaved Bible lay, and carried it away in piecemeal. I perfectly remember the strange pleasure I felt in reading the history of Abraham and of David. I liked mournful narratives, and greatly admired Jeremiah, Ezekiel, and the Lamentations. I pored on these pieces of the Bible in secret for many months, for I durst not show them openly, and, as I read constantly, and remembered well, I soon astonished all our honest neighbours with the large passages of scripture I repeated before them. I have forgot too much of my Biblical knowledge, but I can still rehearse all the names of the patriarchs, from Adam to Christ, and various other narratives seldom committed to memory."

When about seven or eight years old, Alexander was sent to the hills with the sheep, but his father chid him for laziness and uselessness, because he was a bad and negligent herd-boy. The truth was he was a weakly child, and was likewise short-sighted; a difficulty of vision, which wholly unfitted him for a part of his business, and he was naturally of a sedentary and studious turn, very ill-adapted for the vacant indeed—but still vigilant life of a shepherd. His constant devotion to reading, and surprising memory, made him very early the wonder of the rustics among whom he lived, and a wish was entertained that the boy could have "school learning." In all probability the wish would have had no practical result, but for the fortunate event that William Cochrane, his mother's brother, chanced, in the summer of 1783, to pay a visit to his relatives, and being flush of money, which he had earned by travelling about England selling goods, and hearing much of the genius (as it was called) of his nephew, generously offered to put the boy to the New Galloway school, six miles off and to pay for his board while there. He was accordingly sent thither, when in his ninth year, and for a month at least after his appearance, the poor, clownish, self-taught scholar was the laughing-stock of his comrades, who made merry at his uncouth pronunciation and awkward gait. They soon learned to feel differently when, within three months, the stranger stood dux of the Bible class. In the meantime he was taught to write, and was making rapid progress, when a bad illness seized him and compelled him to leave school, which he saw not again for four years.

No sooner was his health somewhat restored than he was again put to his former employment of assisting the rest of the family as herd-boy, at which he continued about three years. During all this time his desire for learning never left him; he spent every farthing he could get from friends or strangers in the purchase of ballads and penny histories, of which he carried bundles in his pockets, and read them in the glen, or on the hill-side while tending the cattle. "My fame," he says, "for reading and a memory was *loud*, and several said I was a living miracle! I puzzled the honest elders of the church with recitals of Scripture and discourses about Jerusalem, &c." In 1787 he borrowed from a countryman, "Salmon's Geographical Grammar," which greatly delighted him, particularly by the specimens it contained of the various languages of the world. He also copied the maps he found in the book, and altogether "got immense benefit" from it.

He was now twelve years of age, and as he could read and write, was engaged by the heads of two families in a neighbouring parish to teach their children throughout the winter. His fees were no more than fifteen or sixteen shillings, with which he bought books of history and arithmetic, one of which was "Cocker's Arithmetic," "the plainest of all books," he says, "from which in two or three months, I learned the four principal rules of arithmetic and even advanced to the Rule of Three, with no additional assistance except the use of an old copy-book of examples, made by some boy at school, and a few verbal directions from my brother Robert; .... my memory now contained a very large mass of historical facts and ballad poetry, which I repeated with pleasure to myself and the astonished approbation of the peasants around me."

The year following, his father was employed to herd, at a place four miles above Minnigaff, at the school of which village Murray resolved to attend and entered himself accordingly, walking thither three days every week during the summer. There he read incessantly, not only using his own books, but, by coming before time, the books of all the other scholars, which were left at the school. At Martinmas 1789, he was engaged by three families in the moors of Kells and Minnigaff, to teach their children, and during the winter he migrated about, remaining six weeks in one family at a time, the families living at considerable distances from each other.

His mind now began to be directed to the subject of foreign languages. His account of the manner in which he proceeded is full of simplicity and interest. "I had read that Homer, Virgil, Milton, Shakespeare, and Newton were the greatest of mankind. I had been early informed that Hebrew was the first language, by some elders and good religious people. In 1789, at Drigmore, an old woman who lived near showed me her Psalm-book, which was printed with a large type, had notes on each page, and likewise what I discovered to be the Hebrew alphabet marked letter after letter, in the 119th Psalm. I took a copy of these letters, by printing them off in my old way, and kept them."

He next began the study of the French Grammar, and, in less than a fortnight he was able to read a little of the language, and then borrowed of one of his schoolfellows, the Latin Rudiments, and by diligent study, and with the help of his master, he beat a class of scholars, who were considerably advanced. All this was the work of about two months and a half before the vacation, and a fortnight after it. During the winter he was, as usual, employed in teaching; but he continued his own studies with the greatest eagerness. Having, among other books, bought an old copy of Ainsworth's Dictionary, for one shilling and six pence, and borrowed a few other books from friends, he proceeds, " I literally read the dictionary throughout. My method was to revolve the leaves of the letter A, to notice all the principal words and their Greek synonyms, not omitting a glance at the Hebrew; to do the same by B, and so on through the book. I then returned from X and Z to A; and in these winter months I amassed a large stock of Latin and

Greek vocables. From this exercise I took to Eutropius, Ovid, and Cæsar, or at times, to Ruddiman's Grammar. The wild fictions of Ovid have had charms for me ever since. I was not a judge of simple and elegant composition; but when any passage contained wild, sublime, pathetic, or singular expressions, I both felt and tenaciously remembered them. Here I got another book which from that time has influenced and inflamed my imagination. This was 'Paradise Lost,' my first acquaintance with which I account an era in my reading. I cannot describe the ardour or various feelings with which I read, studied, and admired this first-rate work."

In the following spring he again returned to school, and from this time, his progress seems to have been rapid, and the advancement he made truly surprising. Finding a schoolfellow in possession of a Greek Grammar, he commenced that language, and having introduced himself to Mr. Maitland, the clergyman of the parish, by writing letters to him in Latin and Greek, he procured from that gentleman the loan of a large number of books which he studied with the utmost diligence. He tells us that his custom was to lay down a new and difficult book when it had wearied him; and to take up another—and then a third—and to resume this rotation frequently, always striving to seize the sense; but when satisfied that he had succeeded in doing so, not wearying himself with analyzing every sentence.

Having, as we have seen, been long acquainted with the Hebrew alphabet, he determined to learn that language, and sent to Edinburgh for a Hebrew Grammar by the postman. By the aid of this he soon mastered the rudiments, and being so fortunate as to procure a dictionary, and shortly after the entire Bible, he "in a few months read the Old Testament throughout, and many passages and books of it a number of times." This summer must (to use his own expression) have been "devoted to hard and continued reading." He had, in fact, chiefly by his own unassisted efforts, made himself familiar with the French, Latin, Greek, and Hebrew languages, and read several important works in all of these within about a year and a half from the time when they were wholly unknown to him.

In the winter of 1792, he got from a friend the loan of Bailey's English Dictionary, from which he learned "a vast variety of useful matters, especially the Anglo-Saxon alphabet, which led the way to the study of the northern languages." In this manner he proceeded, taking advantage of every opportunity for adding to his store of knowledge and even trying his hand at original composition, to which he thus deprecatingly alludes, "I now, in an hour of ignorance and ambition believed myself capable of writing an epic poem. I chose Arthur, general of the

Britons, for my hero, and during the winter, wrote several thousand blank verses about his achievements. . . . . My companions, young and ignorant like myself, approved my verses, but I perceived they were mistaken, for my rule of judgment proceeded from comparison in another school of criticism." The unfortunate poem was, therefore, consigned to the flames, and poor Murray, who felt that his business at school was now completed, and that he needed a larger sphere for the prosecution of his studies, found himself at a loss in what manner to obtain the object of his ambition. In this perplexity, chancing to meet with a MS. volume of German Lectures on the lives and writings of the Roman authors, written in Latin, he determined to translate it, and employed himself in the task during the winter of 1793. The speculation proved a failure, for on offering the work to the booksellers at Dumfries, he found they would not undertake to publish it; nor did a volume of his poems which he next proposed to them meet with better success. During this visit to Dumfries, he says, "I was introduced to Robert Burns, who treated me with great kindness, and told me that, if I could get out to college without publishing my poems, it would be much better, as my taste was young and not formed, and I should be ashamed of my productions when I could write and judge better. I understood this, and resolved to make publication my last resource."

THE POET'S ADVICE. 129

BURNS GIVING ADVICE TO MURRAY.

Such is the account of his early life given by Mr. Murray himself. In the winter of 1794, he went to Edinburgh. He was indebted to a humble friend for his first introduction to the city in which he laid the foundation of that celebrity he afterwards attained. This was a hawker of the name of M'Harg, by whom he was made known to Mr. Kinnear, then a journeyman printer in the King's printing-office. Through the recommendation of the latter he was brought under the notice of the Principal of the University, Dr. Baird, and was examined before several of the professors. His acquirements could not fail to secure for him the patronage of such men, and they immediately procured him the advantages of the University, free of expense, and assured him of such assistance and protection as would enable him to prosecute his studies successfully.

His subsequent progress was comparatively easy. In the course of two years he obtained a bursary or exhibition to the University of Edinburgh, and never relaxing in his pursuit of knowledge, he soon made himself acquainted with all the European languages, and began to form the design of tracing up all the languages of mankind to one source. His acquirements as a linguist recommended him to Constable, the well-known publisher, as a fit person to superintend a new edition of "Bruce's Travels." In the preparation of that work he was employed for about three years; residing chiefly at Kinnaird House, where he had access to the papers left by the traveller. He also contributed to the "Edinburgh Review," and other periodicals.

Having, after a time, decided to enter into the ministry of the Scottish Church, he was appointed, in 1806, assistant and successor to Dr. Muirhead, minister of Urr, in Dumfriesshire, and there, in the enjoyment of domestic happiness and retirement, he discharged the duties of his office, devoting all his leisure hours to his favourite philological studies. In 1812, the professorship of Oriental Literature in the University of Edinburgh became vacant, and great exertions were made to obtain for Mr. Murray the situation which he seemed so specially adapted to fill. The testimonials of his qualifications for the vacant chair, were of the most honourable kind. They came from a host of distinguished names, all bearing warm and deserved tribute to his merits, and they were successful, for he was elected on the 8th July, 1812, and on the 15th, the University conferred on him the degree of D.D.

These honours, so dearly bought and so richly merited, were bestowed on one whose already enfeebled health soon sank beneath the pressure of his ardent and unceasing labours. Although from the time of his election his strength daily declined he continued to teach his classes during the winter, persevering in the preparation and delivery of a course of most learned lectures on Oriental literature, which were attended by crowded and admiring audiences, and at the same time carrying an elementary work through the press, for the use of his students. Quite unconscious of his real situation he thus persisted in his usual engagements, till within a few days of his death, which took place on the 15th April, 1813, in the thirty-seventh year of his age. The event, to himself being wholly unexpected, was sudden. Happy was it for this learned man that he had not delayed till the last hours of life his preparation for another world. He had given evidence that his religion was sincere and earnest. Conscientious and indefatigable, in his ministerial character he was a zealous, evangelical pastor, and preached the gospel with affection and zeal. He had also consecrated his literary acquirements to the service of Christianity. But a few months before his death he had voluntarily offered to write an Essay on the Importance of the Indian Mission, and in particular, on the importance of the translation of the Scriptures into the several languages of India, carried on through the missionaries at Serampore, and spoke of it in terms of unqualified satisfaction. "These men," he said, "have given us more Indian literature during a few years than we have had since the British took possession of the country. They have put it in the power of British scholars to compare the history of India with that of Greece and Rome, to illustrate from an unexpected quarter the languages of Homer and Virgil, to teach as a common dialect, the radical basis of the ten modern languages now spoken in the peninsula; and the principles of which we are enabled to teach if required, in this University—a thing totally impossible a few years since, and certainly due to the industry of the Society."

Had the life of Dr. Murray been prolonged, he would doubtless have made valuable acquisitions to the literature of his country, and his name might have been transmitted to posterity as eminent in the department of Eastern literature, with those of Sir W. Jones, and Dr. Carey, and his colleagues. Enough he did accomplish to obtain for him a place among the most learned philologists, and to entitle him to the admiration of those who regard the task of self-culture as the highest and best to which we can devote our efforts.

Benjamin Franklin.

"One of the most remarkable men certainly of our times as a politician, or of any age, as a philosopher, was Franklin."—Lord Brougham.

THE annals of self-education do not contain a more surprising example than that presented by this most extraordinary man, who, from the position of a poor printer's boy, raised himself by his talents and industry to a distinguished place among his fellow-men. It is not within the limits of these slight sketches to give even a short history of his eventful life. We shall, therefore, attempt no more than to trace its early steps, and learn how he overcame the difficulties that obstructed his path, and bent to his purpose the adverse circumstances, under which most would have succumbed.

Happily, Franklin has himself told the story of his early days, in the form of a letter to his son. He commences it thus:—"From the poverty and obscurity in which I was born, and in which I passed my earliest years, I have raised myself to a state of affluence and some degree of celebrity in the world. As constant good fortune has accompanied me, even to an advanced period of my life, my posterity will perhaps be desirous of learning the means which I employed, and which, thanks to Providence, so well succeeded with me. And now I speak of thanking God, I desire with all humility, to acknowledge that I attribute the happiness of my past life to his divine Providence, which led me to the means I used, and gave me success." Of his ancestors he gives the following interesting account:—" Our humble family had lived in the same village in Northamptonshire (England) on a freehold of about thirty acres, at least 300 years, and how much longer could not be ascertained. This small estate would not have sufficed for their maintenance without the business of a smith, which had continued in the family down to my father's time. They had early embraced the reformed religion, and continued Protestants through the reign of Mary, when they were sometimes in danger of persecution on account of their zeal against Popery. They had an English Bible, and to conceal it and place it in safety, it was fastened open with tapes under and within the cover of a joint-stool. When my great-grandfather wished to read it to his family, he placed the joint-stool on his knees, and then turned over the leaves under the tapes. One of the children stood at the door to give notice if he saw the apparitor coming, who was an officer of the spiritual court. In that case, the stool was turned down again upon its feet, when the Bible remained concealed under it as before."

Benjamin was born at Boston in North America, on the 11th of January 1706, being the youngest, save two girls, of a family of seventeen children. His father had emigrated from England about twenty-eight years before, on account of the persecutions carried on in the reign of Charles II., against the Nonconformists. He was, as his son assures us, a man of sterling worth, sound understanding, and solid judgment, who stood high in the opinion of his neighbours, though, in consequence of the burden of a numerous family, he was never able to do more than maintain himself and his children in respectability. At ten years of age, Benjamin was taken to help at his father's business, which was that of a tallow chandler and soap-boiler, and his employment was "to cut wicks for the candles, fill the moulds for cast candles, attend the shop, and go on errands." These occupations were little to the boy's taste, who had a strong inclination for a sea-faring life, and "living near the water, was much in it and on it," soon learning to swim well, and to manage boats— accomplishments which he turned to good account in after days—and when embarked with other boys, being commonly allowed to govern and act as leader, thus early evincing a master spirit. His father, at length dreading lest he should break loose and go to sea, endeavoured to fix his inclination upon some trade which would keep him on land, and determined to place him with a cutler, but the apprentice fee asked was too high for his scanty resources, and in the end, it was resolved to place the boy with his brother James, who had been bred a printer, and was just set up in that business at Boston. To him, therefore, Benjamin was apprenticed when yet only in his twelfth year, on an agreement to remain with him till he came of age.

One of the principal reasons that had determined his father upon this step was the fondness he had from his infancy shown for books. This inclination had led to his being put to a grammar-school when eight years old, with the intention of bringing him up to the ministry; but though he made the most rapid progress during the few months he remained at school, he was taken away before the end of a twelvemonth, from the inability of his friends to support the necessary expenses. He tells us that so great was his relish for reading, that he spent every penny he could procure in buying books, his first acquisition being Bunyan's works, in separate little volumes. His father's small library consisted almost entirely of works on divinity, which did not interest him much; but he happily found among them "Plutarch's Lives," and a book by Defoe, called, "An Essay on Projects," with another by Dr. Mather, entitled "The Art of Doing Good." "These," he says, "perhaps gave me a turn of thinking that had an influence on the principal future events of my life." To his new occupation of a printer he very readily turned his mind, and in a little time made great progress in the business, and became a useful hand to his brother. "I had now," he says, "access to better books, and was sometimes able to borrow one, which I was careful to return soon and clean. Once I sat up in my chamber reading the greatest part of the night, when the book was borrowed in the evening and to be returned in the morning, lest it should be found missing. After some time, a merchant who frequented our printing-office, took notice of me, and kindly invited me to see his library, and lent me such books as I chose to read. I now took a strong inclination for poetry, and wrote some little pieces. They were wretched stuff—in street-ballad style—but when they were printed, my brother, supposing it might turn to account, sent me about the town to sell them. The first sold prodigiously, being an account of a recent shipwreck, which had made a great noise. This success flattered my vanity; but my father discouraged me, by criticizing my pieces, and telling me verse-makers were generally beggars. Thus I escaped being a poet, and, probably, a very bad one."

He next turned his attention to the composition of prose, of which he afterwards became a consummate master (his correspondence upon business, whether private or on state affairs, being pronounced "a model of clearness and compendious shortness"); and his first attempts were made in a trial of skill with one of his acquaintance, "a bookish lad, named Collins," with whom he carried on a discussion in writing. The papers were shown to Franklin's father, whose natural acuteness and good sense again enabled him to render an essential service to his son, by pointing out to him his deficiency in elegance of expression, method, and perspicuity. From that moment, the youth determined to spare no pains in endeavouring to improve his style, and we have the following account of the method he pursued for that purpose.

"About this time, I met with an odd volume of the 'Spectator.' I had never before seen any of them. I bought it, read it over and over, and was much delighted with it. I thought the writing excellent, and wished, if possible, to imitate it. With this view, I took some of the papers, and making short hints of the sentiments in each sentence, laid them by a few days, and then, without looking at the book, tried to complete the papers again by expressing each hinted sentiment at length, and as fully as it had been expressed before, in any suitable words that should occur to me. Then I compared my Spectator with the original, discovered some of my faults, and corrected them. Sometimes I had the pleasure to fancy that in certain particulars of small importance I had been fortunate enough to improve the method or the language, and this encouraged me to think that I might in time come to be a tolerable English writer, of which I was extremely ambitious."

Even at this early age nothing could exceed Franklin's perseverance and self-denial while pursuing his favourite object of cultivating his mental faculties to his utmost ability. When only sixteen, he chanced to meet with a treatise recommending a vegetable diet, one of the arguments of which immediately caught his attention—namely, its greater cheapness—and he accordingly determined to adopt it, saving, by this means, about half the money it had formerly cost him for food. "This," he says, "was an additional fund for buying of books; and I found another advantage in it. My brother and the rest going from the printing-house to their meals, I remained there alone, and despatching presently my light repast (which was often no more than a slice of bread, a handful of raisins, or a tart, and a glass of water), had the rest of the time, till their return, for study, in which I made the greater progress from that clearness of head and quicker apprehension, which generally attend temperance in eating and drinking." *

Among other works which he read at this time,

---

* Franklin persisted in this vegetarian system for nearly two years, when he relinquished it in the following manner. Chancing one day to be with some fishermen who were catching cod, which they proceeded to cook, he remonstrated with them on what he called "a massacre." "My arguments," he says, "appeared very reasonable; but I had formerly been a great lover of fish, and when it came out of the frying pan it smelt admirably well. I balanced some time between principle and inclination, till recollecting that when the fish were opened, I had seen smaller fish taken out of their stomachs, then, thought I, if you eat one another, I don't see he mentions "Locke on the Human Understanding," and the Port Royal "Art of Thinking;" and he also made himself master of arithmetic, by the aid of Cocker's book on that science, being, as he says, ashamed of his ignorance in figures, which he had twice vainly attempted to learn at school.

At the age of seventeen, Franklin took a step which was eventually the means of introducing him to independence. He had never been on good terms with his brother, who, he thought, treated him with undue severity, while, at the same time, he acknowledges that he was himself also to blame, as he was frequently impertinent and provoking. In consequence of these quarrels, he was perpetually wishing to cut short the term of his apprenticeship, and at length an unexpected opportunity presented itself, of which he took advantage. In his account of the matter, he avows that he acted dishonourably, and in a manner he afterwards regretted. His indentures had, for certain reasons it is unnecessary to detail, been cancelled under a private agreement, that he should still remain bound to his brother's service for the full time. A fresh difference having shortly after arisen, he took advantage of the letter of the law, and resolved to assert his freedom. In conse-

why we may not eat you. So I dined upon cod very heartily, and have since continued to eat as other people, returning only occasionally to a vegetable diet. So convenient a thing it is to be a *reasonable creature*, since it enables one to find or make a *reason* for everything one has a mind to do."

quence of this exploit, his brother took measures to prevent his procuring employment in Boston, and finding no one would engage his services, he resolved to make his way to New York, the nearest place where there was a printer. He accordingly sold his books to raise a little money, and, unknown to his parents, went on board a sloop, and in three days reached the place of his destination, three hundred miles from the home he had quitted. On applying to the only printer likely to give him work, he learned, to his bitter disappointment, he was already supplied with hands; and the only advice he gave him was to proceed to Philadelphia, where he had a son who wanted an assistant. Philadelphia was one hundred miles further; but Franklin had no alternative, and determined to go on. After a disastrous voyage, he at length arrived there in safety, and gives the following striking picture of his adventures:—" I shall be particular in my description of my first entry into that city, that you may compare such unlikely beginnings with the figure I have since made there. I was in my working-dress (my best clothes coming round by sea); I was dirty, from my being so long in the boat; my pockets were stuffed out with shirts and stockings; and I knew no one, nor where to look for lodging. Fatigued with rowing, walking, and the want of sleep, I was very hungry, and my whole stock of cash consisted of a single dollar and about one shilling in copper coin, which I gave

FRANKLIN'S ARRIVAL IN PHILADELPHIA.

to the boatman for my passage. I walked towards the top of the street, gazing about me, till I met a boy with bread. I inquired where he had bought it, and went immediately to the baker's he directed me to. Not knowing the different prices, nor the names of the different sorts of bread, I told him to give me threepence worth of any sort. He accordingly gave me three great puffey rolls. I was surprised at the quantity; but took it, and having no room in my pockets, walked off with a roll under each arm, and eating the other. Thus I went up Market Street, as far as Fourth Street, passing by the door of Mr. Read, my future wife's father, when she, standing at the door, saw me, and thought I made, as I certainly did, a most awkward and ridiculous appearance. Then I turned and went down another street, eating my roll all the way, and coming round found myself against the wharf, near the boat I came in, to which I went for a draught of the river water, and being filled with one of my rolls, gave the other two to a woman and her child that came down the river in the boat with us.

"Thus refreshed, I walked again up the street, which by this time had many clean-dressed people in it, who were all walking the same way. I joined them, and thereby was led into the great meeting-house of the Quakers, near the market. I sat down among them, and after looking round awhile, and hearing nothing said, being very drowsy, through labour and want of rest the preceding night, I fell fast asleep, and continued so till the meeting broke up, when some one was kind enough to rouse me.

This, therefore, was the first house I was in, or slept in, in Philadelphia."

Refreshed by this brief repose, he then went in search of a night's lodging, and the next morning found out the person to whom he had been directed, who was not able to give him employment, but introduced him to another printer, named Keimer, who set him at first to put an old press to rights, and afterwards took him into regular employment. He soon made himself at home in his new situation, formed acquaintance with several young people of the town, who were lovers of reading, with whom he spent his evenings very pleasantly, and gained money by his industry and frugality. He had been some months in Philadelphia, when a brother-in-law, who was the master of a trading sloop, happening to hear of him in one of his voyages, wrote to him in very earnest terms to entreat him to return home. The letter, which he sent in reply to this application, reaching his brother-in-law when he chanced to be in company with Sir Wm. Keith, the governor of the province, it was shown to that gentleman, who expressed considerable surprise on being told the age of the writer, and immediately said, that he appeared to be a young man of promising parts, and that if he would set up on his own account in Philadelphia, where the printers were wretched ones, he had no doubt he would succeed ; for his part he would procure him the public business, and do him every service in his power." These apparently generous offers were afterwards made to Franklin personally, who accepted them with the greatest satisfaction, and, encouraged by the governor's friendship, returned to Boston with letters from his new patron, which he hoped would induce his relatives to furnish him with the necessary funds for carrying out his project. His father, however, withheld his consent, saying, that he considered his son too young and inexperienced to be trusted with the management of so important an undertaking. At length, with the consent and blessing of his parents, he returned to Philadelphia, to endeavour, by diligence and steady conduct, to earn the means of establishing himself in the world. On his arrival he waited on the governor, who, hearing of his father's refusal to furnish him with means, promised he would himself do so, and, after some conversation, advised him to make a voyage to England, to furnish himself there with all necessaries for a new printing office, and make connections in the trade, &c. To this proposal Franklin assented, and after a short delay he sailed, accompanied by a friend named Ralph, somewhat older than himself. On reaching London he presented certain letters (as he supposed) of credit and recommendation, given him by Governor Keith, on which he had relied to procure him patronage and employment. What was his surprise and dismay to find that he had been completely deceived! In the utmost perplexity he made known the whole affair to an American gentleman, who had made the voyage on board the same ship with him, and from whom he learned that the governor was well known to be in the habit of making promises he never intended to keep, and that none who knew his character would have advised him to put any confidence in his professions.

Thus cruelly deceived, the young adventurer found himself unbefriended and moneyless in a strange land. He had no other resource but to endeavour to procure employment at his trade in London, and accordingly applied to a Mr. Palmer, a printer of eminence in Bartholomew Close, in whose service he remained nearly a year. He afterwards procured an engagement with Mr. Watts, near Lincoln's Inn Fields, and here he gave striking evidence of those habits of temperance, self-command, industry, and frugality, which distinguished him through after life. While his fellow-workmen spent a great deal of every week's wages on beer, he drank only water, and found himself much stronger and more able for labour than they on their strong potations. "From my example," he says, "a great many of them left off their muddling breakfast of beer, bread, and cheese, finding they could, with me, be supplied from a neighbouring house with a large porringer of hot water gruel, sprinkled with pepper, crumbled with bread, and a bit of butter in it, for the price of a pint of beer, namely, three-halfpence. This was a more comfortable, as well as cheaper meal, and kept their heads clearer. Those who continued sotting with their beer all day, were often, by not paying, out of credit at the alehouse, and used to make interest with me to get beer, *their light*, as they phrased it, *being out*. I watched the pay table on Saturday night, and collected what I stood engaged for them, having to pay near sometimes thirty shillings a week on their accounts. This, and my being esteemed a good *riggite*, that is, a jocular verbal satirist, supported my consequence in the society. My constant attendance (I never making a *St. Monday*) recommended me to the master, and my uncommon quickness at composing, occasioned my being put upon works of despatch, which are generally better paid, so I went on now very agreeably." After remaining about a year and a half in London, Franklin took leave of England, "where," he says, "I had improved my knowledge, though I had by no means improved my fortune; but I had made some very ingenious acquaintance, whose conversation was of great advantage to me, and I had read considerably."

On reaching Philadelphia he first engaged himself as clerk in a mercantile house, and in the course of a year became the superintendent of Keimer's printing office, where he acquired so much esteem, and so far improved his connections, that he resolved to embark in business for himself. He entered into partnership with a fellow-workman named Meredith, whose friends were able to furnish him with a supply of money sufficient for the concern, which was, no doubt, very small, for Franklin has recorded the high degree of pleasure which he experienced from a payment of five shillings only, the first fruits of their earnings. "The recollection," he touchingly remarks, "of what I felt on that occasion, has rendered me more disposed than otherwise I might have been, to encourage young beginners in trade." His habitual industry and undeviating punctuality obtained him the notice and business of the principal people in the place. He instituted a club, under the name of "the Junto," for the purpose of the discussion of political and philosophical questions, which proved an excellent school for mutual improvement. All the members of this association exerted themselves in procuring business for him, and one of them, named Breinthal, obtained from the Quakers the printing of some folios of a history of their society. "Upon these," says Franklin, "we worked exceeding hard, for the price was low. . . . . . . It was often eleven at night, and sometimes later, before I had finished my distribution for the next day's work, but so determined was I to continue doing a sheet a day of the folio, that one night, when having imposed my forms, I thought my day's work over, one of them, by accident, was broken, and two pages (the half of the day's work) reduced to *pie*; I immediately distributed and composed it over again before I went to bed, and this industry, visible to our neighbours, began to give us character and credit." The consequence was that business, and even offers of credit, came to them from all hands. Shortly after they ventured to set up a newspaper, which Franklin's efforts as writer and printer caused to succeed, and they also obtained the printing of the votes and laws of the Assembly. In process of time Meredith withdrew from the partnership, and Franklin met with friends who enabled him to take the whole concern on his own hands, and add to it the business of a stationer.

Thus, about the year 1729, when he was only in the twenty-fourth year of his age, he found himself, after all his disappointments and vicissitudes, established in business, and with at least a prospect of well-doing before him. With what care and diligence he proceeded to establish his credit as a good tradesman he tells us:—"I took care not only to be in *reality* industrious and frugal, but to avoid the appearances to the contrary. I dressed plain, and was seen at no places of idle diversion: I never went out a-fishing or shooting; a book, indeed, sometimes beguiled me from my work, but that was seldom, private, and gave no scandal; and to show that I was not above my business, I sometimes brought home the paper I purchased at the stores through the streets on a wheelbarrow. Thus, being esteemed an industrious, thriving young man, and paying duly for what I bought, the merchants who imported stationery solicited my custom; others proposed supplying me with books, and I went on prosperously." So prosperously that in the following year he ventured to marry a lady to whom he had been engaged before he left for England. It was a happy union: Franklin thus characteristically speaks of their domestic *menage*, "We have an English proverb that says—

> ' He that would thrive
> Must ask his wife.'

"It was fortunate for me that I had one as much disposed to industry and frugality as myself. She assisted me cheerfully in my business, folding and stitching pamphlets, tending shop, purchasing old linen rags for the paper-makers, &c. We kept no idle servants, our table was plain and simple, our furniture of the cheapest. For instance, my breakfast was for a long time bread and milk (no tea), and I ate it out of a twopenny earthen porringer, with a pewter spoon: but, mark how luxury will enter families, and make a progress in spite of principle. Being called one morning to breakfast, I found it in a China bowl, with a spoon of silver! They had been bought for me without my knowledge by my wife, and had cost her the enormous sum of twenty-three shillings, for which she had no other excuse or apology to make, but that she thought *her* husband

THE SILVER SPOON.

deserved a silver spoon and China bowl as well as any of his neighbours." What woman will not pronounce Mistress Franklin justified in her deed?

"This (continues he) was the first appearance of plate and china in our house, which afterwards, in course of years, as our wealth increased, augmented gradually to several hundred pounds in value."

From this point of his history, Franklin's career in the pursuit of fortune and independence was (as is well known) eminently successful. Unceasing industry, business-like habits, a large fund of disposable talent, general information and readiness in the use of his pen, either for amusement or instruction, gradually secured to him a large circle of friends, and raised him from poverty to affluence. He engaged in literature, established a circulating library, the first ever known in America; wrote a paper to advocate a paper currency, and, in 1732, first published his celebrated "Poor Richard's Almanac," of which the distinguishing feature was a series of maxims of prudence and industry in the form of proverbs. It was continued for twenty-five years, and is said to have reached the circulation of ten thousand annually. These maxims, collected together and called "The Way to Wealth," obtained uncommon popularity, and have been translated into various languages.

It has been truly remarked that Franklin's turn of mind was eminently practical. Science in his hands always was applied directly to the uses of common life; and, while he never neglected his own affairs, industry and economy of time enabled him to originate, or take an active part in supporting a variety of projects for the public good. His political career began in 1736, when he was appointed clerk to the General Assembly of Pennsylvania, an office which he held for several years, till he was at length elected a representative.

As a philosopher, Franklin's name is indissolubly linked with the history of electricity, in which he was one of the most active, patient, and successful experimenters, and his industry was rewarded by that brilliant discovery, the corner-stone of his scientific fame—the identity of the electric fluid and lightning. He had long entertained the idea, but did not prove it till 1752. An accident came to his assistance. One day his attention was drawn to a kite which a boy was flying, and it suddenly occurred to him that here was a method of reaching the clouds. Soon after, seeing a thunder-storm approaching, he went, accompanied by his son only, to a shed, where, having raised his kite, he fastened a key to the lower extremity of the hempen string, and then, insulating it by attaching it to a post with a piece of silk, he waited the result. The cloud passed over, but for some time no signs of electricity appeared; at length, however, Franklin observed some loose threads of the string rise and stand erect, exactly as if they had been charged with electric fluid. He immediately presented his knuckle to the key, and to his inexpressible delight, drew from it

FRANKLIN PERFECTING HIS GREAT DISCOVERY.

the well-known spark. It is said that his emotion was so great at this completion of a discovery which was to make his name immortal, that he heaved a deep sigh, and felt that he could willingly have paid for his discovery with his life.

Here we must take our leave of Franklin. As a politician and patriot his fame vies with that which he acquired as a great and original philosopher, and "the poor printer's boy, who, at one period of his life, had no covering to shelter his head from the dews of night, rent in twain the proud dominion of England, and lived to be the ambassador of a commonwealth which he had formed, at the court of the haughty monarchs of France who had been his allies." He attained the advanced age of eighty-four years and three months, expiring on the 17th April 1790.

William Hutton.

WILLIAM HUTTON, author of "The History of Birmingham," and various other works, was in all respects a self-taught genius, and the history of his life, written by himself when in his seventy-fifth year, is a most remarkable piece of autobiography, affording an instructive example of how, by indomitable energy, perseverance, and application, it is possible for a man to overcome the disadvantages of the most neglected youth and adverse circumstances.

He was born in the town of Derby in the year 1723, and was the second son of a journeyman woolcomber, in very humble circumstances. To the burden of a numerous family were added other and heavier drawbacks, for although a man of good natural abilities, Hutton's father was indolent and prone to drinking, consequently his poor wife and children suffered the greatest distress. William relates that more than once he had known his unhappy mother, an infant on her knee, and three or four others about her, obliged to fast from morning till night, and when at last food was procured, he saw her with tears relinquish her share of the scanty repast to satisfy her clamorous babes. Such scenes engrave themselves deeply upon the young heart, and for his mother he ever retained the tenderest recollection. She was not, however, long spared to solace his childish woes; for when he was in his tenth year she died, unable longer to sustain the sad struggle with misery and want. Her loss was a real calamity to her children, while their father, apparently made reckless by distress and misfortune, gave himself up to evil ways, and squandered his scanty earnings, leaving his orphan family to shift for themselves. A more deplorable picture than that drawn by William of his condition it is difficult to conceive: "My mother gone, my father at the alehouse, and I among strangers, my life was forlorn; I was almost without a hope, and nearly naked. At one time I fasted from breakfast one day till noon the next, and even then dined upon flour and water only, boiled into a hasty pudding." The only education he ever received was during his fifth and sixth years, when he was sent to school to "a Mr. Thomas Meat, of harsh memory, who often," he adds, "took occasion to beat my head against the wall, holding it by the hair, but never could beat any learning into it: I hated all books but those of pictures." At seven years old his days of toil commenced, for he was sent to work at a silk mill, and being the youngest and smallest of the juvenile work-people employed there might, one would imagine, have excited some feelings of compassion, but no mercy was shown him. Being too short of stature to reach the engine, they fastened a pair of high pattens upon his feet, which the poor child was compelled to drag about with him for a year. "I had now," he says, "to rise at five every morning, submit to the cane whenever convenient to the master, and be the constant companion of the most rude and vulgar companions, never taught by nature, nor ever wishing to be taught." On one occasion he was beaten so violently that a sore formed on his back and threatened mortification; in fact he carried the scar to his dying day. During seven long years his servitude at this drudgery continued; at length in his fourteenth year it terminated, and, much against his inclination, he was again bound apprentice for seven years more to a brother of his father, who was a stocking-weaver at Nottingham. He had now to work hard for small remuneration, and it being the custom for apprentices at this trade to procure clothes by over-time work, he had an additional motive for using his utmost exertions, for he was just at the age when vanity begins to stir in the young heart, and he "envied every new coat he saw," longing to earn one for himself. Three long years, however, passed before he could save enough to purchase a decent suit, and meanwhile he had a still more powerful incentive, which he mentions in a manner that shows his acquaintance with hardship and rude companions had failed to corrupt his morals, and that the pure springs of affection were unsullied in his bosom. "Perhaps there is not," he writes, "a human being but sooner or later feels, in some degree, the passion of love. I was struck with a girl, watched her wherever I could, and peeped through the chink of the window-shutter at night. She lay near my heart eleven years; but I never spoke to her in my whole life, nor was she ever apprized of my affection." This may be thought an improbable statement; the experience it records is certainly not unique. Such examples of the poetry of passion, though rare, do still occur, even amid the most apparently prosaic influences.

William's uncle appears to have been a sensible and industrious man, but he was stern and harsh, and occasionally violent in temper; the result was frequent disputes between him and his nephew; and at length they came to a complete rupture. On the week of the Nottingham races the young man had wrought a day less than usual, and had, in consequence, failed to complete a piece of work given him to do. "Could you have completed it?" asked his uncle. Ever truthful, William replied, in a low and meek voice, "I could." On receiving this reply his enraged employer, forgetting all moderation and decorum, flogged him most severely. Stung with the disgrace, and unable to endure the contempt of his comrades, who sneered at his mortification, he watched an opportunity and fled, taking his clothes with him in a bundle, and two shillings in his pocket. His account of what he endured during a week's wandering is truly affecting. Without object or hope he went in the direction of Birmingham. By the wayside he parted for a few moments from his bag, which was stolen, and in great distress he reached that city, " little thinking that nine years later he should become a resident there, and after the lapse of more than thirty years should write its history." In vain he endeavoured to procure work there; everybody to whom he applied pronounced him to be a runaway apprentice, and " would have nothing to say to him." Starvation was the only alternative, and he found himself compelled, in his utter destitution, to appeal to the compassion of his father. The matter ended in his return to his uncle's house, and a mutual treaty of forgiveness and forbearance was entered into, and kept.

There is something highly characteristic of the keen discernment and courageous spirit of Hutton in the account he has given of his first view of the great city which was afterwards to be the scene of his success in life, and of which he was to become the distinguished chronicler. A wearied and homeless wanderer, friendless and forlorn, he reminds one of Whittington gazing wistfully upon the mighty

Babel, when we read his description of his first sight of Birmingham from Handsworth Heath. He had never seen more than five towns before, and this one far excelled them all. Hunger and misery were forgotten as he beheld,—"charmed with the beauty of St. Philip's church,"—which first caught his eye, and amazed at the elegance of the buildings in the suburbs. "I was surprised at the place," he says, "but more at the people. They possessed a vivacity I had never beheld. I had been among dreamers, but now I saw men awake. Their very step along the street showed alacrity. Every man seemed to know what he was about. The town was large and full of inhabitants, and these inhabitants full of industry. Their appearance was strongly marked with the modes of civil life; the weather was extremely fine, which gave a lustre to the whole; the people seemed happy, and I the only animal out of use."

This was the morning picture: in the evening he thus portrays himself: "I sat to rest upon the north side of the old Cross, near Philip Street; the poorest of all the poor belonging to that great parish of which, twenty-seven years after, I should be overseer. I sat under that roof, a silent, oppressed object, where, thirty-one years after, I should sit to determine differences between man and man. Why did not some kind agent comfort me with the distant prospect?"

HUTTON'S FIRST EVENING IN BIRMINGHAM.

The young man's second apprenticeship expired in 1744, and he then continued to serve his uncle as a journeyman. He seems now first to have evinced a disposition for the cultivation of his intellect and taste. His earliest predilection was for music, and to this amusement he devoted all his leisure hours. It is interesting to read of the skill and ingenuity he evinced in the pursuit of this object. Not having money enough to purchase an instrument, he thought of making one. He borrowed a dulcimer, and even before learning to play upon it, set about fabricating one like it; but he had neither timber to work upon nor tools to work with; and what then? He tells us, " Necessity, 'tis said, is the mother of invention. I pulled a large trunk to pieces, one of the relics of my family; and as to tools, I considered that the hammer key and the plyers belonging to the stocking frame would supply the place of hammer and pincers. My pocket-knife was all the edge tools I could raise; and a fork with one limb was made to act in the double capacity of sprig awl and gimlet." With these sorry implements he at last fashioned the dulcimer which, after learning to play upon it, he sold to one of his companions for sixteen shillings, bought a coat with the money, and constructed a better instrument.

It was not till he had reached his twenty-third year that Hutton began to take a liking for books. His earliest purchase—three volumes of the "Gentleman's Magazine,"—was made in 1746, and this gave rise to a new application of his ingenuity. His treasures were in a tattered and filthy condition, and he determined to rebind them with his own hands, and having carefully watched a bookbinder at his work, he contrived to learn enough of the craft to accomplish his purpose. Of this man he bought several cast-off tools, and among other things an old binding press, which had been put away for *firewood*. " Having considered the nature of its construction, I paid him two shillings for it, and then asked him for a hammer and a pin, which he brought with half a smile and half a sneer. I drove out the garter pin which, being galled, prevented the press from working, and turned another square, which perfectly cured the press. This proved for forty-two years my best binding press."

After the death of his uncle in 1745, Hutton, seeing no prospect of getting a competency in the stocking trade, which at that time was in a very depressed condition, resolved to seek for some new employment. This cost him a painful struggle, and he ingenuously confesses that on one occasion when speaking on the subject, he was so much affected that he burst into tears, to think he should have been seven years apprenticed to a trade by which he could not earn bread.

He now went to live with his sister, a woman of sterling character and worth, in whose strong sense and unwearying affection he found his greatest solace and help in this time of his utmost need. His thoughts were now turned upon the matter of a new trade, and his great desire was to become a bookbinder. "Everybody scoffed at the idea," he says, "except my sister, who encouraged and aided me, otherwise I must have sunk. I considered that I was naturally of a frugal temper; that I could watch every penny, and live upon little; that I hated stocking making, and that if I continued at the frame I was certain to be poor ; if I ventured to leave it, I could but be so." Partly from the novelty of a stocking maker turning bookbinder, and partly to reward his merit in having taught himself, many people gave him volumes to bind, and by-and-by he found it necessary to go to London to buy better tools. His sister managed to raise him three guineas for this purpose, and with this sum sewed into his shirt collar he started for London ; he walked fifty-two miles the first day, and spent fivepence ; the rest of the journey was performed with equal economy ; and having bought three alphabets of letters, a set of figures, some tools, leather, and boards, he returned to Nottingham at the end of nine days.

Thus provided, he determined, with the approval of his stanch friend and counsellor, to open a shop at Southwell, a place fourteen miles distant, intending to go there on market days, which were the Saturdays. He accordingly took a shop, put up a few shelves in it, sent some dozens of old books, and became in one day "the most eminent (because the only) bookseller in the place." His life during his winter of Southwell shopkeeping is thus described : "I set out at five every Saturday morning, carried a burden (tools, &c.), of from three pounds weight to thirty, opened shop at ten, starved all day upon bread and cheese and half a pint of ale ; took from one shilling to five shillings, shut up at four, and by trudging through the solitary winter night and the deep roads five hours more, I arrived at Nottingham by nine, where I always found a mess of milk porridge by the fire, prepared by my excellent sister." Well might he add, "Nothing short of a surprising resolution and rigid economy could have carried me through this."

This humble attempt was, however, the beginning of his prosperity. Next year he was offered about two hundred pounds weight of old books on his note of hand, for twenty-seven shillings, by a dissenting minister, to whom he was known, and upon this he immediately determined to break up his establishment at Southwell and to remove to Birmingham. He did so, and succeeded so well, that by never suffering his expenses to exceed five shillings a week, he found at the end of a year he had cleared about £20. This encouraged him to venture on a larger shop at a rent of £8. Here he continued to prosper by unremitting prudence and industry, and five years after, when he had accumulated £200, he married the niece of a neighbour, Mr. Grace. The match was one of mutual affection, and it is truly delightful to find him, after a union of forty-one years, thus referring to their reciprocal affection: "I told her that she never had approached me without diffusing a ray of pleasure over my mind, except when any little disagreement had passed between us; she replied, 'I can say more than that; you never appeared in my sight, even in anger, without the sight of you giving me pleasure.' I received the dear remark, as I now write it, with tears."

His wife's portion was £100, and by the death of an uncle she afterwards inherited £200 more; and with such an accession to his means, Hutton was persuaded to buy a quantity of paper, and hang out a sign "The Paper Warehouse;"—"from this small hint," he says, "I followed the stroke forty years, and acquired an ample fortune."

Yet he was not without his reverses, occasioned by a natural desire to increase his gains too rapidly. With the hope of adding a maker's profit to a seller's, he expended a large sum in building a paper mill; but after many years of toil and anxiety, he was compelled to sell it at a considerable loss. He, however, learned wisdom by experience, and turning actively to his old trade, to use his own expression, "struck the nail that would drive." With sagacious as well as honest thrift, he went on the principle of never borrowing. "I could not bear," he tells us, "the thought of living to the extent of my income; never omitted to take stock, and regulated my annual expenses so as to meet casualties and misfortunes."

And now, for many years, he continued pursuing his business with persevering steadiness, observing, in his memoirs, "When life glides smoothly on, incident is not to be expected. The man who sleeps in peace has no tale to tell. Trade was successful, my family in a prosperous state, we enjoyed our little pleasures, and lived happily." Hutton was a fond father; he worked willingly for his wife and children, as is proved by this admirable remark, "Attention will increase business, and it was not possible to avoid attention, for the pleasure of providing for a beloved family is inconceivable." He had many children, some of whom survived, but several died in infancy. His grief for their loss appears to have been uncommon and injurious to his health; while, on the other hand, his delight in those who survived was proportionally great. In everything he undertook Hutton seems to have manifested the same energetic spirit and persevering activity; while building a house for himself in the neighbourhood of Birmingham, he was "up at four in the morning, setting the people to work, watching and labouring with them all day, and frequently charged himself with the meanest and most laborious parts of the employment." This was after he had been twenty-five years in business. Again, having soon after engaged in farming (by which he lost a considerable sum), he tells us that he visited his farm three or four times a week, always on foot, though it was four or five miles distant, and, having arrived there by five in the morning, he was back to Birmingham for breakfast. At the same time he acquitted himself with credit, in the discharge of various civic offices, and, having been appointed a commissioner of the Court of Requests, distinguished himself greatly by his zealous and able exertions in performing the duties of that office.*

In the midst of his multifarious engagements, Mr. Hutton conceived the idea of becoming an author, and in 1780 composed his well-known " History of Birmingham," the first work which came from his pen. He spent, he tells us, nine months in writing it, and he published it in the spring of 1782. The enjoyment he took in his task is apparent in the following words, " Pleased as a fond parent with this history, as my first literary offspring, I may be said, while in manuscript, to have had the whole by heart. Had a line been quoted, I could have followed it up through the chapter. Frequently, while awake in the night, I have repeated it in silence for two or three hours together, without adding or missing a word." When speaking of another of his works he remarks that the pen brings its own reward for its labour in the pleasure of writing. Immediately on the appearance of this work, Hutton was elected a Fellow of the Antiquarian Society of Edinburgh. A second edition was called for in the following year, and it has ever since retained its reputation as an admirable topographical production. Its author was

---

* In one of his works entitled, "The Court of Requests," Mr. Hutton has given an entertaining collection of anecdotes illustrative of the proceedings in which he took so important a part. In the preface, he says, " I may be said to have spent a life upon the bench, which, though without profit, carried its own reward; for I have considered the suitors as my children, and when any of this vast family looked up to me for peace and justice, I have distributed both with pleasure."

HUTTON AND HIS DAUGHTER ON AN EXCURSION.

nearly sixty years of age when it was written, but he lived to add to it a long list of other works. The last of these, his "Description of the Roman Wall," was written at the advanced age of seventy-eight, and, in order to gather the materials for it, he undertook and performed a journey of six hundred miles, entirely on foot. His daughter, who accompanied him on horseback, wrote a very pleasing account of this excursion. Another of the works of his old age was a volume of Poems; verse-making seems to have afforded him the sweetest solace, and to have been the chief relaxation of his leisure, especially after he had given up business on reaching his seventieth year.

In 1791 occurred the dreadful riots at Birmingham, of which Mr. Hutton has left a narrative full of intense indignation of feeling, and both interesting and curious for its graphic detail of those atrocious proceedings, alike disgraceful to the mad perpetrators and to the inhabitants who suffered such frightful outrages to be committed, day after day, without resistance. Among the sufferers he was himself one of the principal, his houses and property in Birmingham being destroyed, as well as his country house at Bennet's Hill, which the rioters pillaged and burned to the ground. He was obliged to fly with his wife and daughter, the former in a dying condition, and was compelled literally to implore shelter from strangers, while yet doubtful whether anything remained to them in the world of all they had so recently called their own. It was not until the troops were at length brought up to terminate the scene of riot, that he found it safe to return. He reckoned his actual loss to be above £8000, of which he recovered only £5390.

Mrs. Hutton had suffered severely from the alarm she had experienced, and her state became increasingly painful. Much of her husband's time was now occupied in bestowing the most tender cares upon the beloved companion of his life. "My practice," says the kind-hearted old man, "was to rise about five, relieve the nurse of the night by holding the head of my dear love in my hand, with the elbow resting on the knee. At eight, I walked to business at Birmingham. When I returned, I nursed her till eight, amused myself with literary pursuits till ten, and then went to rest."

In 1796, she died, and five years after that event, he thus describes his life, " I rise at six in the summer, and seven in winter, march to Birmingham, where my son receives me with open arms; I return at five in the afternoon, and my daughter welcomes me with a smile; I then pass the evening in reading, conversation, or study, without any pressure upon the mind, except the remembrance of her loss."

This remarkable man died in 1815, at the great age of ninety-two. He had the happiness of being respected and esteemed in his latter years, and took great pleasure in recalling the past, and retracing, in imagination, his path through life. His daughter, who completed his autobiography, says, "My father recollected, with gratitude to Providence, the success that had crowned the exertions of his youth; 'How thankful ought I to be,' he would say, 'for the comforts that surround me. Where should I have been now if I had continued a stockinger? I must have been in the workhouse. They all go there when they cannot see to work. I have all I wish for. I think of these things every day.' I think, (she adds), the predominant feature in my father's character was his *love of peace*. No quarrel ever happened within the sphere of his influence in which he did not act the part of mediator. The first lessons he taught his children were that the *giving up an argument was meritorious;* and *that having the last word was a fault.* In conclusion she thus sums up his character, "He was an uncommon instance of resolution and perseverance, and an example of what these can effect."

Joseph and Stephen Montgolfier.

ON the 5th June, 1783, the small town of Annonay, situate at thirty-six miles from Lyons, was in a state of extraordinary excitement. Two brothers, named Montgolfier, had promised to exhibit a balloon ascension; an unheard of thing—incredible, as most thought. At the appointed hour a crowd gathered in the public square of the place, eager to witness the novel spectacle. Nothing, however, was visible but immense folds of paper 110 feet in circumference, fixed to a frame weighing about 500 pounds, and containing 22,000 cubic feet (French measure). To the great astonishment of all it was announced that this balloon would be filled with gas, and would rise to the clouds, which very few could believe. On the application of fire underneath, the mass gradually unfolded and assumed the form of a large globe, striving, at the same time, to burst from the arms which held it. At length it rose with great rapidity, and in less than ten minutes was at 1000 toises of elevation. It then described a horizontal line of 7,200 feet, and gradually sank.

This balloon contained nothing but heated air, maintained in a state of rarefaction by a fire, the receptacle of which was attached underneath the globe of paper, which had an orifice opening downwards. Machines on this principle were called *Montgolfiers*, to distinguish them from the hydrogen balloons which were made immediately afterwards.

The news of this phenomenon quickly flew to Paris, where it excited admiration mingled with surprise. The members of the Academy of Science resolved immediately to repeat the experiment at their own expense and on a larger scale. Subscriptions were accordingly made for the construction of a balloon of vast dimensions. M. Charles, a celebrated professor of experimental physics, and Robert, a mechanician, were charged with the management of the design. After a careful investigation of all Montgolfier's details, M. Charles substituted silk, covered with gum, for linen and paper. The gas employed by the Montgolfiers was produced by burning straw and wool under the balloon, this appeared to him so dangerous, that, in its place, he made use of hydrogen gas.

On the 27th August of the same year, less than three months after the Annonay experiment, an immense crowd assembled in the Champ de Mars, and waited impatiently for the ascension of the monster machine. The air resounded with repeated acclamations. The balloon, first balancing itself at the height of five or six feet from the ground, soared aloft, and in two minutes gained a height of 1000 metres, and, ascending rapidly to a prodigious height, alighted, in its downward course, at a village five leagues distant from its starting point.

Shortly after, Stephen Montgolfier went to Paris, and repeated, in the presence of the court at Versailles, the exhibition of Annonay, with a machine constructed on the same model, and inflated by the same means. While he is thus engaged we will give the reader a sketch of the history of these two brothers to whom we owe the invention of balloons.

Joseph and Stephen Montgolfier were paper-manufacturers, living at Annonay, where their father had for many years carried on this business, bringing up a numerous family. Joseph, born in 1740, seems to have been a somewhat self-willed boy, very impatient of control, and difficult to manage. He was placed at school at Tournon with two of his brothers, but showed an insuperable dislike to the regular habits and discipline enforced there. When only thirteen years old he resolved to run away, his plan being to get to the sea-shore, where he supposed he might pick up a living upon the shell fish he should collect. Hunger arrested the young truant's steps at a farm in Lower Languedoc, and there, for a while, he earned his bread by gathering leaves for silk-worms; but before long, his parents, being made acquainted with his proceedings, discovered his hiding-place, and, in consequence, he was soon captured and carried back to school. The distaste he had always felt for study was vastly increased when a theological course was proposed in addition to the other instructions he received. Fortunately a treatise on arithmetic fell into his hands at this time, and immediately he devoured it with eagerness. The methodical inductions which the science of numbers require, were, however, by no means adapted to the turn of Montgolfier's mind, and he preferred to grope his way to the desired end by a method of his own, —a species of mental arithmetic constructed after his peculiar fashion, in which, all his life long, he delighted, and by means of which he contrived occasionally to solve the most intricate problems of geometrical science.

Prompted by his passion for independence, he quitted his native town and went to St. Etienne, in Forez, where he took up his abode in an obscure retreat, and subsisted, for some time, upon the produce of his skill in fishing, while he carried on a variety of chemical experiments, and manufactured Prussian blue and various salts useful for manufacturing purposes, which he himself hawked about in the villages of the Vivarais.

Weary, after a while, of his self-imposed solitude, he went to Paris, where he made acquaintance with numerous scientific men, and passed some time in their society, until recalled by his father, who desired that he would come and share with him the management of his paper manufacture. Montgolfier was desirous to put in practice his numerous schemes for improving various branches of the paper making; but to this the old man, naturally prejudiced in favour of the old and established methods by aid of which he had secured a good measure of prosperity in his business, refused his consent. These new-fangled ideas found no favour with him, and Joseph, associating himself with two of his numerous brothers, commenced two new establishments at Voiron and Beaujeu. There his inventive genius had full scope; but his hazardous speculations and want of practical experience, together with his natural indifference, were inimical to his interests as a man of business, and his affairs became involved. He, however, extricated himself from this temporary difficulty, and continued, with even increased ardour, his eager research for scientific discovery. His labours were completely successful. In conjunction with his brother, he eventually made great alterations in the manufacture of common and of coloured and tinted papers; contrived an air-pump for rarefying the air; and introduced several chemical and mechanical improvements. It is said by his biographer that he anticipated the invention of stereotype plates, and the hydrostatic press. At length his ingenuity was directed into a new channel, which speedily rendered his name famous throughout Europe.

180 THE FIRST CLUE.

MONTGOLFIER WATCHES THE ASCENDING SMOKE.

There have been numerous stories related as to what gave the first clue to the idea of such a machine as the balloon. According to some, the thought was suggested to Stephen by the waving of a shirt which was hanging before the fire, in the warm and ascending air. Others assert that it was Joseph who first caught the notion by watching the smoke as it ascended the chimney one day, during the memorable siege of Gibraltar, while he sat solitary and musing on the possibility of penetrating into the place, to which his attention had been called at the moment by an engraving of it that hung upon the wall. These tales are probably but partially true. It is known that the younger brother, Stephen, had been much impressed by the perusal of Priestley's work upon the different kinds of air; and it is said that on his way home from Montpelier, where he had purchased that book, he conceived the idea of navigating the heavens by means of a gas lighter than common atmospheric air. He reflected upon this idea, and anticipating its possible results, exclaimed, "Now we may journey in mid air!" A notion so extravagant, as it would have been pronounced by most others, found eager reception with Joseph, to whom it was instantly communicated—for the two brothers were tenderly attached to each other, and sympathized in all their tastes and pursuits. Their subsequent calculations, experiments, and proceedings, were all carried on in common, and neither would allow the merit of ultimate success was due to him more than to his fellow-labourer. Such truly fraternal co-operation is delightful to witness, and does honour to the hearts of these ingenious men.

After all, as it has been well observed, " we owe the invention of balloons to one of two accidents— either to that of philosophers being paper-makers, or to that of paper-makers being philosophers." The brothers had both studied natural philosophy and chemistry, and their business gave them facilities for procuring large masses of light envelopes. Stephen, like his brother, was not brought up to their father's business, but only entered upon it after the death of the eldest son of the family. He was five years younger than Joseph, and had, when very young, been sent to Paris, where he learned Latin and mathematics, and studied, as a profession, architecture, under a skilful master. The very moderate allowance made him by his father was entirely expended by him in the purchase of books and mathematical instruments, and materials for experiments. He even devoted to the same purpose the money he received for the plans which he was employed to make, and in this way industriously accumulated knowledge, employing the talents he had already gained for the acquisition of new information. Being employed to build the small church of Faremontier, which had been destroyed by fire at the period of the Revolution, he came under the notice of an excellent patron of the arts, M. Réveillon, who soon became his attached friend, and entrusted to him the erection of a new manufacture which he was about to establish in that village; and at a subsequent period, in the eagerness of his friendship, he actually sacrificed his fine gardens at the Faubourg St. Antoine, appropriating them for the purpose of making the first aerostatic exhibitions.

Stephen Montgolfier was wholly absorbed in the pursuit of his business as an architect, when he, in turn, was summoned by his father to undertake the superintendence of the manufacture at Annonay. He returned home, young in years, but with a mind stored with ideas, matured and chastened by experience. Though not yet thirty years old, his hair was already white. His varied knowledge was soon brought to bear upon the business to which he now devoted his attention, and before long, the fruits of his management were visible in the increased prosperity of the establishment. Several new machines; a variety of ingenious contrivances for simplifying the processes of manufacture; improvements in the articles required for the various operations carried on; plans borrowed from the English and Dutch workshops; in short, all that skill and science could bring to bear upon his work, he had recourse to. But *the* invention by which his name was to be immortalized appears to have been at first originated by reflection upon the above-mentioned treatise of Priestley. Assisted by Joseph, he speedily commenced a succession of experiments; and at length, after various

THE MONTGOLFIERS INVENTING THE BALLOON.

suggestions, the thought struck them that as the elevation of the clouds was attributed to the presence of electric matter, and as it appeared, from certain experiments, that electrified bodies were diminished in weight, it might be possible to accomplish their purpose by means of electricity. After trying numerous methods, they applied fire underneath a balloon, "as well to increase the layer of electric fluid upon the vapour in the vessel, as to divide the vapours into smaller molecules, and dilate the gas in which they are suspended." It appears from their expressions, which are somewhat obscure, that they thought they were imitating a cloud, by electrifying the gases and vapours contained in the atmosphere. The experiment succeeded, and a balloon of 23,000 cubic feet (French) was raised with considerable force.

As has been already said, the first public experiment was made at Annonay, with complete success. It is unnecessary to relate the various repetitions of the experiment made at Paris, previously to the time when men trusted themselves to this novel and hazardous conveyance. The first persons who ventured to leave the earth entirely were the Marquis d'Arlande and M. Pilâtre de Rosier. They performed this feat at the Château de la Muette, near Passy, in November 1783. The particulars of this, the most interesting of all aerostatic voyages, were given with minute detail in the *Procès Verbal* as follows:—

" . . . . The machine being filled, set off at fifty-four minutes past one—the marquis and M. P. de Rosier being in the car. It rose in the most majestic manner; and when it was about 270 feet high, the intrepid voyagers took off their hats and saluted the spectators. No one could help feeling a mingled sentiment of fear and admiration. The voyagers were soon undistinguishable; but the machine, hovering upon the horizon, and displaying the most beautiful figure, rose at least 3000 feet high, and remained visible all the time. It crossed the Seine below the barrier of La Conférence, and, passing thence between the Ecole Militaire and the Hôtel des Invalides, was in view of all Paris. Satisfied with their experiment, and not wishing to travel further, the voyagers agreed to descend; but seeing that the wind was carrying them upon the houses of the Rue de Séve, they preserved their presence of mind, increased the fire, and continued their course through the air till they had crossed Paris. They then descended quietly on the plain beyond the new boulevard, without having felt the slightest inconvenience, and having in their car two-thirds of their fuel. They could, then, have gone three times as far as they did go. They occupied from twenty to twenty-five minutes in their journey. The machine was 70 feet high, 46 feet in diameter, it contained 60,000 cubic feet, and carried a weight of from 1600 to 1700 pounds."

There follows a list of eight names of spectators, among which is that of Benjamin Franklin.

The second voyage was that of M.M. Charles and

Robert, just at sunset, December 1, 1783, from the Tuileries, in a hydrogen balloon of 26 feet diameter. After coming down, M. Charles re-ascended alone, and was soon 1500 toises high, or nearly two miles. He saw the sun rise again; and as he says, " I was the only illuminated object, all the rest of nature being plunged in shadow." A small balloon launched by Montgolfier, just before the ascent, was found to have run a totally different course, which first gave rise to the suspicion of different directions in the currents of air at different heights.

The third voyage, from Lyons, in January 1784, was made in the largest *Montgolfier* yet constructed, by seven persons, among whom was Joseph Montgolfier. A rent in the balloon caused it to descend with great velocity; but no one was hurt.

These ascensions were indeed, very perilous, and required great caution. Charles's method was considered superior to that of Montgolfier; nevertheless, the latter had many partisans, at the head of whom was M. Pilâtre, who shortly after, venturing to cross, with a Montgolfier, from Dover to Calais, fell a victim to his own temerity; for the covering of the balloon took fire, and the unhappy man, half-burnt, was precipitated to the ground, near Boulogne, and killed. This melancholy event gave a decided preference to the other balloon.

It is very interesting to know that the ideas of Joseph Montgolfier, as to the possible use of his invention, have that character of simplicity and soundness which distinguish the philosopher from the mere projector. He says, "Large balloons might be employed for victualling a besieged town, for raising wrecked vessels, perhaps even for voyages, and certainly in particular cases, for observations of different kinds; for reconnoitring the position of an army, or the course of vessels at twenty-five or even thirty leagues distance, &c. One of these ideas was not long after put in practice at the battle of Fleurus, where the French made a reconnoissance, and prevented a surprise, by means of a balloon.

The merits of the brothers Montgolfier were generally acknowledged, although there were not wanting detractors, who sought to diminish their credit as original inventors, by suggesting that the idea was no novel one, and that mechanicians had long before contrived flying-machines, while philosophers had laid down the principles of which they had availed themselves in the construction of their balloons. Certain, however, it is that though the art of flying had been diligently studied, or at least, discussed for ages, the exceedingly simple contrivance of the Montgolfiers had not been tried, nor even mentioned, by any of the projectors, many of whom were men of ingenuity. Unquestionably he must be considered as the true inventor of the balloon who first raised a mass of solid substance to some considerable height in the air. The French Academy of Sciences recognized the merits of the Montgolfiers, by placing them in the number of their correspondents. A medal was struck in their honour, bearing their effigies, and Stephen, being presented at court, was decorated with the riband of St. Michel. As this honour could not be divided, he obtained for Joseph a pension of 1000 francs, and accepted for his aged father letters of nobility which he had refused for himself. A sum of 40,000 francs was voted by the government for further experiments, and Louis XVI. transmitted that sum to Montgolfier. All proceedings of the sort were, however, speedily arrested by the outbreak of the Revolution. During that disastrous period Joseph kept himself retired, pursuing in seclusion his favourite researches, and he appears to have escaped the notice of the turbulent spirits then dominant.

Stephen was less fortunate, probably his engagements as a master manufacturer attracted attention. He was, during the Reign of Terror, denounced on more than one occasion, and only escaped arrest, which was equivalent to a sentence of death, through the attachment felt for him by his numerous workmen. He is represented as having been a man of simple and amiable character, free from vanity, and indifferent to popular applause, while at the same time he was deeply sensible of the esteem and admiration testified towards him by the most distinguished men of science of his day.

Though he himself escaped the terrible fate of the

guillotine it appears his spirits never recovered from the shock they sustained by the sufferings and death of many of his friends and acquaintance. The calamities of his country had touched him to the heart; a profound melancholy undermined his health, and it was evident that he could not rally. Conscious he should not long survive he removed to Lyons with his family, and having carefully arranged his domestic affairs, he set off alone for Annonay, desiring to spare his wife and children the anguish of a last farewell. As he had doubtless foreseen, he expired, during the journey, in the month of August 1799.

Joseph Montgolfier survived his brother eleven years. The observant eye of Buonaparte did not pass him by without an approving glance. When, as first consul, he distributed Crosses of Honour to those citizens who had contributed to the advancement of the national arts and sciences, Montgolfier received the decoration. At a later period he was appointed administrator of the Conservatory of Arts and Trades. In 1807 he took his place among the members of the institute, and it was he who, during a walk into the country with four of his friends, first proposed the idea of the Society for the Encouragement of the National Industry.

Joseph Montgolfier was simple and plain in his style, and there was an occasional abstractedness and apparent indifference of manner about him which gave him somewhat an eccentric air. He was very ready

JOSEPH RECEIVING THE CROSS OF HONOUR.

to communicate his ideas concerning science and art in conversation with friends, but showed a decided indisposition to commit them to writing. Probably he knew well the limitations of his powers, and wisely adhered to his own course. He died on the 26th June, 1810.

Whether his discovery will ever have any practical value; whether it will ever be possible for men to guide their course through the "shining tracts of air," and rival the bird in swiftness and certainty of flight, is, to say the least of it, problematical; but not the less has the inventor of the balloon a claim upon our admiration, from the ingenuity and steadfast perseverance he displayed in working out his idea.

Philip Matthew Hahn.

THIS remarkable man, called by one of his countrymen the honour of the Duchy of Wurtemburg, was born in 1739, near Stuttgard, in the village of Scharnhausen, where his father was the Protestant minister. When no more than eight years old the boy showed a passion for astronomy and painting. Without any assistance he studied a planisphere which he had found among his father's books, and when but ten years old he could reckon precisely the hours of the rising and setting of the fixed stars. From a treatise on gnomonics which accidentally fell into his hands, he learned how to construct sun dials. Unaided by any instructor he perseveringly practised painting, and his portraits, despite of all their defects, were considered excellent likenesses. He was, however, soon compelled to relinquish this pursuit, for the smell of the paint and varnish occasioned him a serious illness.

At the age of seventeen, this intelligent and industrious lad quitted his boyhood's home. He was desirous to follow his father's sacred calling, and went

A YOUNG STUDENT.

as a theological student to the University of Tubingen. The same tastes he had so early manifested continued to form his delight, and during the hours of recreation, when he was at liberty to follow the bent of his inclinations, he carried on his experiments and researches in company of a fellow student like-minded with himself, named Schandt, who shared his pursuits, and assisted him in making astronomical and optical instruments. Small indeed were the resources at their command. Hahn's father had a family of eight children, and a very limited income, and it was utterly impossible that he should provide the funds requisite for the expensive education needed by a youth of such varied abilities. In consequence our student was put to the greatest shifts: for example, having determined to make himself master of the mathematical works of Wolf, he found himself compelled to copy them, for want of money to purchase the volumes. At another time, in his eagerness to study the mechanism of a watch, he was contented to live for several months on bread and water only, that he might be able to save the sum necessary for the purchase of one. The youthful reader will sympathize with his delight when he found himself in possession of the dearly purchased treasure. He was incessantly pulling his watch to pieces and putting it together again until he knew every wheel and pin in it by heart.

A youth of ability, industry and virtuous habits is generally susceptible to the gentler emotions of our nature; and while yet a student Hahn fell heartily in love. A fair young maiden of the city of Tubingen charmed him into a temporary dream of ambition and delight. She was in a position so far above his own that it was folly to aspire to her hand; yet the very possibility that he might some day distinguish himself and become worthy of her attachment, served as a spur to all his energies, and made him inwardly resolve that he would aim high and strive nobly. This was to love after an heroic fashion; and we cannot but admire the impassioned enthusiast, when we read that, from that time he pursued with redoubled ardour all his studies, and that he strove successfully to attain the utmost development of all his powers.

For a considerable time he devoted himself to the solution of that famous problem which has vainly employed the mathematicians of two thousand years—the theory of a perpetual motion. Perhaps few, if any, have prosecuted it with greater earnestness and more self-denying attention than did Hahn. Compelled by duty to devote all his time daily to his professional studies, he cut short his hours of repose in order to pursue this alluring and longed for object of research. For three weeks, while this fever was at its height, he did not even once lie down to sleep!

So careful was he, at the same time, not to infringe upon the proper duties of his calling, that he distinguished himself during his theological course, as an uncommonly diligent and promising student, and before leaving college was appointed successively, to three different curacies. Our interest in him is, however, principally as an ingenious inventor and mechanist. He next turned his attention to the invention of an instrument for taking the longitude at sea, and of a car set in motion by a steam-machine; but he had not the funds necessary for completing his experiments.

In 1761, during a brilliant summer night, the sight of the starry heavens inspired him with the idea of constructing a machine to represent the motions of the celestial bodies. Ignorant that anybody had attempted such an one before, he commenced his calculations and having been appointed to the pastorate at Onsmettingen, in 1764, he engaged a weaver, a clever maker of wooden clocks, to come to him, and employed him to execute, under his directions, a clock whose movements communicated with a disc, upon which the sun, moon, and principal fixed stars rose and set throughout the year, at the hour indicated by the astronomical observations, at the same time the sun and moon performed their course upon the zodiac and the crescent, and various phases of the latter planet were seen accurately represented.

Anxious to prosecute his experiments with machines better adapted for his purposes than a wooden clock, and finding himself in need of a more skilful workman to aid him, he engaged his early college friend, Schandt, to come and settle near him, offering him the situation of schoolmaster in his parish. Schandt had learned from some workmen of Wurtemburg, who were deaf and dumb, to work in copper and steel, and he had succeeded in perfecting himself in the art. He executed, under Hahn's direction, a very complicated small astronomical machine, a cubic socle (or stand), upon the sides of which were seen various descriptions of dials, a dial-sphere, and a calendar for eight thousand years was surmounted by a movable celestial globe upon which were executed the apparent motions of all the planets and fixed stars. Charles Eugéne, Duke of Wurtemburg, to whom this machine was given, returned it to its owner, on the promise that

HAHN DESCRIBING AN ASTRONOMICAL MACHINE.

he should execute another more complete and larger, and at the same time presented him with a sum of three hundred florins. Accordingly Hahn did construct, within the space of six months, a new and more complete machine, which was placed in the public library of Louisbourg, and was described, at the command of the duke, by the professor and librarian, Vischer.

After having completed this machine he destroyed the original one. The duke, charmed with the skill and intelligence of this great mechanical genius, loaded him with marks of his approbation, and was desirous that he should take professional honours; but Hahn preferred to retain his post as a humble village pastor. He was subsequently appointed to a more lucrative cure, and transferred to the church of Kosnwestheim in the neighbourhood of Stuttgard.

Being now in possession of a comfortable income, his first thought was to recompense, with generous hand, his friend and co-labourer, Schandt, whom no persuasions could induce to quit his beloved village charge. Hahn now summoned to his assistance, two of his brothers, surgeons by profession, but who were taught, under his instructions, to work in copper and steel. He employed them in the construction of a new astronomical clock. Shortly after, his attention was given to the subject of an arithmetical machine, upon the plan of that made by Leibnitz, which he proposed to make more perfect. In order to accomplish this project he entered again into friendly co-operation with Schandt, who, yielding to his wishes, went to him and remained sufficiently long thoroughly to comprehend his ideas, and then, returning to his village, constructed two new machines according to the plans they had devised, and, keeping one for himself, sent the other to his friend.

At the suggestion of the duke Hahn presented his

to the Emperor Joseph II., during the sojourn of that prince at Stuttgard. The monarch thought it very ingenious, and desired that it should be recommended to the notice of the different academies. But Hahn, ever eager after greater attainments, already felt dissatisfied with his work, and had devised new improvements. He therefore took to pieces and partly destroyed his first machine, and for a long time deferred publishing any description of it, laying aside his proposed ameliorations during many months, his attention having been diverted from this subject by the composition of certain theological works which he was then putting to press. At length, in compliance with the earnest solicitations of the celebrated poet, Wieland, he published in the German *Mercury* of 1774, a history and minutely detailed description of his invention. He afterwards had calculating machines constructed, which were much less expensive than the large arithmetical ones, and by the aid of which the largest sums in addition could be instantly cast.

It would not be possible, in this short sketch, to enumerate all the mechanical improvements, especially in the art of horology, which his countrymen owed to the genius of Hahn. After his decease all the instruments of his invention were taken to London by one of his friends, and sold there to great advantage.

The exceedingly temperate and regular life led by

this admirable man preserved him in excellent health for many years, but the excessive labours of his early life, and his unceasing mental activity, brought on by degrees a general exhaustion of the vital powers. He was unwilling to yield to the influence of disease, and thinking himself re-established, persisted in continuing his accustomed efforts; but his strength failed, he fell, apparently, into a continuous sleep, and exhausted nature, gently and painlessly, ceased to perform its functions. He expired on the 2nd May, 1792, in the fifty-second year of his age.

There is great satisfaction in the belief that this inquiring mind, which had so delighted in searching out the evolutions of the heavenly bodies, had yielded its first and highest homage to Him who had endowed it with such uncommon powers of investigation. His piety was practical and simple, and, as a preacher, his exhortations are said to have been almost childlike in their character, being adapted to meet the necessities of his flock. In his published discourses and other theological works he appears to have shown a tendency towards the opinions of the mystic writers. By all his associates he was held in high and deserved veneration for his moral excellence and unblemished integrity. Among his writings were several treatises on his astronomical and other machines, a volume of yearly sermons, beside a translation of the New Testament in German, with a commentary in two volumes.

Robert Gooch.

AS an example of steady industrious application, highly creditable to the man, and deserving of respect and imitation, a notice of Robert Gooch may suitably find a place in these sketches. The circumstances of his boyhood were by no means of the most promising nature. He was born at Yarmouth, in Norfolk, in 1784. His father, who commanded a vessel in the merchant service, possessed very limited means; and his son was denied the advantages of a classical education. He was sent to a day-school, kept by a Mr. Nicholls, where he learned writing and arithmetic. It does not appear there was anything remarkable about him, or indicative of unusual ability; he was a kind-hearted active boy, rather feeble in health, and (a proof of his amiable disposition) a great favourite with the associates of his school-days.

It was determined by his friends that he should adopt the medical profession; and, when about fifteen years old, he was apprenticed to a surgeon and apothecary of his native town. It was about

THE STUDENT AND THE SKELETON.

this time that he commenced the study of Latin; and, without any assistance, he taught himself to read that language with tolerable ease. We catch an interesting glimpse of him at this period of his life, in a private paper written by his own hand. "From the age of fifteen to twenty-one," he says, "I was apprenticed to a country surgeon; and when I had nothing else to do, no pills to roll, nor mixture to compose, I used, by the advice of my master, to go up into my bed-room, and there, with Cheselden*

---

* Author of an admirable work on the Bones.

before me, learn the anatomy of the bones, by the aid of some loose ones, together with a whole articulated skeleton, which hung up in a box at the foot of my bed. It was some time before I overcame the awe with which I used to approach this formidable personage. At first, even by daylight, I liked to have some one in the room with me during my interviews with him; and at night, when I lay down in my bed and beheld the painted door which enclosed him, I was often obliged to make an effort to think of something else. One summer night, at my usual hour of retiring to rest, I went up to my bed-room; it was in the attic storey, and overlooked the sea, not a quarter of a mile off. It was a bright moonlight night, the air was sultry, and after undressing, I stood some time at my window, looking out on the moonlight sea, and watching a white sail which now and then passed. I shall never have such another bed-room; so high up, so airy, and commanding such a prospect; or, probably, even if I had, it would never again look so beautiful, for then was the springtime of my life, when the gloss of novelty was fresh on all the objects which surrounded me, and I looked, with unmingled hope, upon the distant world. Now—but I am rambling from my story. I went to bed; the moonlight which fell bright into my room showed me distinctly the panelled door, behind which hung my silent acquaintance. I could not help thinking of him—I tried to think of something else, but in vain. I shut my eyes, and began to forget myself, when, whether I was awake or asleep, or between both, I cannot tell,—but suddenly I felt two bony hands grasp my ancles and pull me down the bed : if it had been real it could not have been more distinct. For some time, how long I cannot tell, I almost fainted with terror ; but when I came to myself I began to observe how I was placed ; if what I had felt had been a reality I must have been pulled half-way out of the bed ; but I found myself lying with my head on my pillow, and my body in the same place and attitude as when I shut my eyes to go to sleep. This is the only proof I ever have had that it was not a reality, but a dream."

How important in the influence they exert upon the future conduct of the man are the intimacies formed in early youth ! An accidental acquaintance with a gentleman named Harley, which commenced during his apprenticeship, appears to have been the turning point in the mental history of this young man. Gooch's biographer has thus described the friend to whom he was so much indebted. "Mr. Harley was about thirty years of age, and nearly blind ; he was fond of reading, and from the state of his eyes dependent upon others for his literary enjoyments. His studies were miscellaneous—history, chemistry, sometimes medicine, and very often metaphysics. Gooch used to pass most of his evenings in reading aloud to Mr. Harley. Amongst the books so read were Bishop Berkeley's works, Hartley, and Hume's Essays. Mr. Harley used to discuss the subjects of their reading with his young friend, and being a man of acute intellect, he called into action those faculties of mind in which the youth was by nature most gifted. At a comparatively early age he became accustomed to reason on abstract questions, and to take nothing for granted; unquestionably, this was not without its disadvantages and dangers; but had it not been for this intimacy Gooch might, perhaps, have neglected altogether the cultivation of his reasoning powers at the time of life when that cultivation is most important."

So deeply was he impressed with this conviction that he always felt grateful to Mr. Harley, paid him every attention during life, and bequeathed him £100 at his death as a proof of his regard. It is delightful also to know that, when after an absence of many years Gooch revisited Yarmouth, his consideration towards this early instructor and friend was most striking. On the evening of his arrival he expressed his eagerness to call upon him; and when it was suggested that it was both late and dark, he exclaimed that he could find the house blind-fold. Accordingly he groped his way down those narrow curious *rows* so peculiar to Yarmouth, and in due time reached his destination, when he recognised with delight the old broken brass knocker still remaining unchanged.

While Gooch was serving his apprenticeship the attack upon Copenhagen took place; and on the return of Lord Nelson the wounded were conveyed to the Naval Hospital at Yarmouth. Though then but a lad, in consequence of his acquaintance with some of the young surgeons, he was frequently at the hospital. In a letter written long afterwards, he says, " I was at the Naval Hospital at Yarmouth on the morning when Nelson, after the battle at Copenhagen (having sent the wounded before him), arrived at the roads, and landed on the jetty. The populace soon surrounded him, and the military were drawn up in the market-place ready to receive him; but making his way through the dust and the crowd, and the clamour, he went straight to the hospital. I went round the wards with him, and was much interested in observing his demeanour to the sailors. He stopped at every bed, and to every man he had something kind and cheering to say. At length he stopped opposite a bed on which a sailor was lying who had lost his left arm close to the shoulder-joint, and the following short dialogue passed between them. *Nelson*—' Well, Jack, what's the matter with you?' *Sailor*—' Lost my left arm, your honour.' Nelson paused, looked down at his own empty sleeve, and said, playfully, ' Well, Jack, then you and I are spoiled for fishermen; cheer up, my brave fellow!' And he passed briskly on to the next bed; but these few words had a magical effect upon the wounded tar,

NELSON AND THE WOUNDED SAILOR.

for I saw his eyes sparkle with delight as Nelson turned away and pursued his course through the wards."

How admirably was the conduct of the great

commander on this occasion adapted not only to benefit his men, but to teach an invaluable lesson to a lad like Gooch. It did not fail of its effect, as we shall presently see by the conduct he himself pursued when professionally engaged in the hospital.

Owing to the limited circumstances of Gooch's family, aggravated by the detention of his father in a French prison, it was no easy matter to find the requisite funds for the completion of his education and his establishment in life. Great sacrifices were made by his mother and an aged aunt in order to send him to the university at Edinburgh. He arrived there, landing from a Leith smack, in the month of October 1804; poor fellow! his prospects were not of the most encouraging. His means were very scanty, and he knew no one in this novel region save one of his school-boy acquaintances, Mr. Henry Southey, a young man, some twelvemonths his senior, the brother of the poet Southey, who was then a student at the college. They had always been intimate associates, and it was no small comfort to a youth, remarkably shy, and quite unaccustomed to the world, to find a friendly hand outstretched to greet him under such forlorn circumstances.

A few weeks reconciled him to his situation, and seldom did any one enter upon his academical studies with a more fixed determination to profit by the advantages afforded him. We are told that, during the first season, he rarely, if ever, missed a lecture;

he attended the Royal Infirmary, and became a member of the Medical and Speculative Societies. In these societies he very soon acquired the power of expressing himself with facility. "He spoke much better the second year than the first, and before the end of the third session few men were more formidable debaters."

At the end of the first season he passed in Edinburgh, Gooch returned to Yarmouth, and spent part of his vacation at Norwich, where he formed an attachment to a lady who subsequently became his wife. Returning to Edinburgh, in the course of the following winter he felt the first symptoms of indisposition, accompanied by depression of spirits, to which he was ever afterwards occasionally liable. The summer of 1806 he passed in Norfolk: and, whilst he was at Yarmouth, the French Frigate, *La Guerriere*, was captured and brought into the roads by the *Clyde*, and the sick and wounded of both vessels were sent ashore to the hospitals. The extraordinary number of patients was too much for the ordinary staff of medical attendants, and Gooch was requested to assist them. He afterwards told the following anecdote to a friend:—"Among my patients was a French soldier, who had received a splinter wound in the leg, which had split the principal bone up to the knee, and produced violent inflammation of the joint: his constitution after a time beginning to give way it was thought necessary to sacrifice his limb in order to save his life, and it was accordingly amputated above the knee-joint. The stump did well, and all danger from this quarter was at an end; but from long lying on the back the flesh upon his loins began to ulcerate. With much difficulty I lifted the poor fellow upon his side: he was sadly wasted, and lest his hips should suffer in the same way I had him moved from side to side. It required a great deal of care and contrivance to prevent him from returning to his old position; but the difficulties were overcome, and all pressure being removed from the wounds, I had the pleasure of seeing them become healthy and begin to heal. But the time was now come for me to leave the hospital and deliver my patients into other hands.

"At the end of a fortnight I returned to Yarmouth to take ship for Edinburgh, and of course walked down to the hospital to see how Pierre and my other patients were going on. His eye happened to be on the door as I entered the ward; he immediately caught sight of me, and clasping his hands with a cry of joy, turned his face upon the pillow and burst into tears. He knew I was to return on my way to Edinburgh,—he had been looking for me every day, —he felt that he should die, and now he said that he should die happy. During my absence he had become dreadfully altered, and looked as if he would soon verify his own prognostic. He had not been neglected; had received the ordinary attention of a naval hospital; but his situation required more. He had been suffered to lie constantly on his back, and the consequences had been such that his constitution had sunk rapidly. He was wasted to a skeleton, had become irritable and low-spirited, and did nothing but cry over his sufferings, and regret the loss of my attendance. The nurse said he had been continually talking of me; he had amused himself with writing French verses about me, and was never so cheerful as when he had his slate in his hand and was working at his poetry. I am glad I returned when I did, for the poor fellow died the night after. The affair affected me a good deal; I shall never forget it; and I have often regretted that I did not defer my journey in order to see him fairly through the dangers of his illness."

It is not possible to read this narrative without feeling one's heart glow towards the young man who was so keenly sensitive to the sufferings of his helpless patient, and so self-denying in his attendance upon a case requiring so much care. And how affecting the gratitude of the poor Frenchman!

In June 1807, Gooch took his degree of doctor of medicine; and in the ensuing winter, feeling the desirableness of fitting himself for the various branches of the medical profession, he determined to pass a season in studying anatomy and surgery in London. He accordingly became a pupil of the celebrated surgeon, Astley Cooper, and diligently carried out his object. During the following year he commenced the career of a physician at Croydon, where he speedily attained considerable practice, and laid the foundations of his subsequent success; many of his country patients being afterwards useful to him when he removed to the metropolis.

It is not within the scope of this slight sketch to give more than a general notice of Dr. Gooch's subsequent history. It pleased God to visit him with a heavy affliction in the loss of his wife, who died in less than three years after their marriage. It appears that this trial was made useful to him in the highest and best sense. He sought consolation where it is never sought in vain, by looking up to the Hand that had afflicted him, acknowledging his dependence, and seeking mercy from the only true source of help and solace. His home being thus rendered desolate, and finding himself, in point of circumstances, somewhat better off, he resolved to remove to London as his permanent residence. His high moral and intellectual worth secured for him the friendship and patronage of many who were both able and willing to assist him in his profession. In 1812 he was elected physician to the Westminster Lying-in Hospital,—a situation which secured to him first-rate advantages, and afforded him great opportunities of acquiring practical knowledge in the various branches of the healing art. He soon began to find his prospects brighten, and assured his friends that practice was coming in upon him in a way and with a rapidity which surprised him. Indeed he felt reason to anticipate that he should soon be beyond the reach of pecuniary cares. In one of his letters to a friend there is the following curious and interesting passage, which gives a striking idea of the contrivances to which an ardent zeal occasionally has recourse. "I have been attending the daughter of one of the most zealous methodists I have ever met with; he never gives me a fee but I find written in red ink on the bank-note some religious sentence. I have now two of these curiosities lying by me; on one is written, 'Who shall exist in everlasting burnings?' on the other, 'The wages of sin is death.' There were several others which I cannot remember. I have sent them out into the world to do all possible good, and these will soon follow them."

In 1814 Dr. Gooch married a second time; his domestic happiness was secured by this union, and every year added to his reputation and increased his income. There was but one serious drawback to his progress; this was the state of his health, which became so much impaired as to occasion himself and his friends the greatest uneasiness. Feeling that his life would probably be short, he was desirous to do what he possibly could for his family, and as much as was permitted him for the benefit of his fellow-men. In "religion and strenuous exertion" he found consolation and relief amidst bodily suffering and family bereavement, but he said—and let the reader mark and seriously ponder the statement,—" Whosoever says that the latter is the chief, says false; for the former affords support when the mind is incapable of exertion! it tranquillizes in moments which exertion cannot reach, and is not only not the least, but the best of the two."

The death of a favourite child and his own ill health naturally directed his thoughts and hopes towards the eternal world; and well for him was it that he was gradually weaned from earth, for his course was soon run, and his sun went down while it was yet noon. He died in the forty-sixth year of his age, but not before he had accomplished much, and won a reputation worthy of a man of honourable ambition and high principle.

His activity of mind prompted him to be always at work; and whatever he engaged himself upon, there was an earnestness of purpose which not unfrequently exhausted his feeble powers. In the latter years of his life he exhibited a striking contrast between mental vigour and bodily weakness.

His friendly biographer concludes with this tribute to his memory as a man and a physician:—" Enough has been said to show that Robert Gooch was no ordinary man. During a short life, embittered by almost constant illness, he succeeded in attaining to great eminence in his profession, and left behind him valuable contributions to medical knowledge.

. . . . "His manners were singularly well adapted to a sick room,—natural, quiet, impressive; and the kindness of his heart led him to sympathize readily with the feelings of others, and rarely failed to attach his patients strongly. Those who were accustomed to rely upon him merely for professional aid found it difficult to supply his place; to his intimates and his family his loss was irreparable."

Christian Gottlob Heyne,

PROFESSOR OF ELOQUENCE IN THE UNIVERSITY OF GOTTINGEN.

THE life of this eminent scholar affords a highly instructive and encouraging lesson to all who devote themselves to study under disadvantageous circumstances. Although, during his latter years, he enjoyed an extraordinary distinction in his own country and throughout Europe, he was, even up to mature manhood, subject to an unusual amount of poverty and privation. Born amid the miseries of the lowest indigence, he successfully struggled against adversity, which to him was doubly painful, because he was naturally endowed with great sensitiveness and tender feelings.

Of his juvenile years he has himself given a deeply touching narrative. "My good father, George Heyne," he says, "was a native of Silesia, but his lot fell in those days when the Protestants in that country were exposed to the persecutions of the Romish Church. My father on this account forsook his paternal abode, and strove to support himself in Saxony by the labour of his hands. 'What shall it profit a man if he gain the whole world and lose his own soul?' was the idea which the scenes of his youth had most deeply impressed upon his mind. No favourable accident ever occurred to promote his plans and assist his efforts to improve his circumstances. A series of misfortunes gradually reduced him so low, that his old age was embittered by the pressure of indigence.

"I was born and educated in the deepest poverty.* The earliest companion of my infancy was want, and the first impressions were those made by the tears of my mother, who knew not where to find bread for her children. How often did I see her, on a Saturday, with streaming eyes, wringing her hands, when she had been endeavouring to dispose of the produce of her husband's incessant labour (he was a linen-weaver), and was obliged to return without having found a purchaser.

"My parents did what they could, and sent me to a school in the suburbs, where I acquired the character of learning everything very quickly, and took great pleasure in learning. So early as my tenth year, I had, in order to pay for my own schooling, instructed a neighbour's child in reading and writing. I had learned all that could be acquired in the ordinary routine of the school; and Latin was taught only in private lessons, for which a whole groschen (about three-halfpence English) would have been

---

* He was born at Chemnitz, a small town of Saxony, in 1729.

HEYNE RELATING GOOD NEWS TO HIS MOTHER.

required weekly, and that sum my parents could not afford. I had a godfather, a baker, in good circumstances, to whom I was sent one Saturday for a loaf—and I entered the shop with streaming eyes. He inquired what I cried about. I told him the cause of my affliction, and he promised to pay the weekly groschen for me, on condition that I should come every Sunday and repeat all that I had learned by heart out of the Bible.

"Intoxicated with joy, I ran off with my loaf, which I kept tossing up into the air, at the same time leaping up, barefoot as I was. No wonder my loaf tumbled into a puddle. This mishap recalled me to my senses. My mother rejoiced at the good news which I brought; but my father was not so well pleased. Thus two years passed away, and my schoolmaster declared, what I had long known, that he could teach me nothing more. The time was now come for me to leave school and take to the calling of my forefathers. It was natural that my father should wish to have an assistant at his laborious occupation, and that my aversion to it should give him great displeasure. I was as anxious, for my part, to continue my studies at a grammar-school; but the means were totally wanting.

"My second godfather was a minister in the suburbs, who, at the recommendation of my schoolmaster, sent for me, and, after examination, told me I should go to the grammar-school at his expense. Who can conceive the transports I felt? I was referred to the head-master, examined, and placed, with commendation, in the second class. Of a weakly constitution, oppressed with want and misery, cut off from the sports and enjoyments of childhood, I was very small for my age; and my schoolfellows, judging from my appearance, formed a very mean opinion of me."

At this school many obstacles were thrown in his way. His clerical godfather, although he paid for his instruction, was so niggardly that he refused to furnish him with the necessary books, so that he had to borrow them as he best could from the other boys. The instruction, too, was by no means of the best kind; and he might, he says, have probably sunk into confirmed stupidity, had he not been accidentally roused from his dull lethargy by a curious accident. One of the superintendents, at an examination of the pupils, suddenly asked if any of them could tell what anagram might be made out of Austria. None of them knew what an anagram was, so the querist had to explain the meaning of the word; and then, after a little reflection, Heyne produced the word *Vastari*. Great was the surprise of the superintendent; the more so as he saw before him a little urchin on the lowest form of the second class. He was loud in his commendations. Heyne, after relating this pedantic adventure, as he calls it, adds, "It gave, however, the first impulse to my powers. I began to feel confidence in myself, and to raise my head, in spite of all the contempt and hardship under which I languished."

On leaving school the young ardent student complained that he was a perfect novice in all relating to classic literature, having read scarcely a few chapters of Livy, and being a stranger to the auxiliary sciences of geography, history, &c.

During the last year there had been a faint glimmering of hope for him. A superior master was engaged; and had he been in favourable circumstances and able to avail himself of the private lessons of this tutor, he felt he should have done much; but here again his poverty and adverse fate checked his hopes. The cruel treatment of his penurious godfather, and the displeasure of his father, who still thought that the lad had neglected the call of duty in refusing to follow his trade, added to the constant pressure of want, suffered no sweet day-dreams to visit his young bosom, and cast a gloom over all his feelings. With bitter lamentation he complained—"Reserved, shy, and awkward in behaviour, where was I to acquire politeness, a right way of thinking, or any means of improving either my heart or my understanding?" The very sense of his deficiencies was a proof of the latent power and feeling within him; and, indeed, he adds, "Nevertheless a sense of honour, a wish for something better, an anxiety to raise myself above my low condition, incessantly accompanied me."

Just at this period he was fortunate enough to obtain a situation as tutor in a family where he was kindly treated; and though the remuneration was very small, it enabled him, with the aid of what he earned by private lessons, to give a trifle to his parents.

At length the time approached for him to go to the University of Leipsic; but where was he to find the means? All his hopes reposed upon the old clergyman, who sent him, under the escort of his curate, to the longed-for place, but was more than ever close-fisted. It was only by constant dunning he contrived to procure a few dollars from the stingy old man, whose wretched doles were accompanied by reproaches and insults. The consequences of so much distress were very painful: a deep depression overspread his mind, and it was with difficulty he kept himself from despair. "One single kind heart," he says, "I found in the servant of the house, who daily laid out her own money to supply my wants, and risked almost all she had when she saw me reduced to such extreme necessity. Did I but know where to find this good, tender creature, with what pleasure would I repay her kindness to me!" How touching is this incident, and how full of instruction to the humblest individual, who may, perchance, like this poor serving-maid, find means to do good, and to shed a ray of comfort across the path of some noble child of misery. Hail to thee, nameless benefactress of Heyne, the learned scholar! Verily thou shalt have thy reward.

At the close of his first year at college, Heyne became acquainted with one of the professors, who showed him some kindness, and urged him to apply to the study of the ancient classics. At this time such was his application to study, that for above half a year he allowed himself only two nights' sleep in a week, until he was attacked with a fever, which nearly proved fatal. Meanwhile his necessities increased to the utmost pitch.

The time having arrived when, his academic studies being completed, he had to choose his future career, he had but two resources—the profession of an advocate, or that of a private teacher. Chance at length decided the matter. A poem which Heyne had written in memory of M. Lacoste, the minister of the French Protestant Church in Leipsic, attracted the notice of one of the nobility at Dresden, who expressed a wish to become acquainted with the author. Letters were sent, desiring him to go to Dresden without delay; and, following the advice of his friends, he did so; but, alas! only to meet with a cruel disappointment. For some time he was fed with hopes that he should obtain a good appointment, but it all ended in his being dismissed without place or money.

Imagine what must have been the condition of a young man in the capital without funds, without credit, without acquaintance! He must have starved had he not procured an engagement as tutor to a young gentleman for a few months, at the end of which time he was again left without resources. His distress now increased to such a point that he began to sell his books to buy bread; and not unfrequently empty pea-shells, which he collected and boiled, were his only meal. As for lodging, he had none. A lad whom he had formerly known took compassion upon him, and received him into his room; but there was no bed for him, and he had and religion became the subjects of my daily meditation, and I began to live and act upon principles of which I had not thought before. My feelings were exalted to a high degree of innocent enthusiasm." As might have been expected, the tender passion was soon kindled; nor were his feelings unshared by the lady, whose name was Theresa Weiss.

This short season of happiness was soon interrupted by the inroads of the war. Heyne was compelled to leave Wittenberg, and for a considerable time wandered about, at a loss what course to pursue. Having returned, in the summer of 1760, to Dresden, he was present during the bombardment of the city by the Prussians. His situation was perilous in the extreme. "I passed several nights with others in a cellar, and the days in my room, where I could hear the balls from the battery whiz past the windows. Such an indifference to danger and to life itself took possession of my soul, that on the morning of the last day I went to bed, and, in spite of the most tremendous noise of balls and bombs, slept soundly till noon. When I awoke I hurried on my clothes, ran down stairs, and found the house deserted. The house door was fastened. At length I jumped out of the window into the street; the thoroughfares were full of fugitives; and, together with the crowd, I ran, amidst a shower of balls, to the New Town, which the Prussians had just left. Happy in being able to get shelter, I passed one part of the night on the bare stones, and in the other I beheld the awful spectacle of falling bombs and a burning city. At daybreak a little gate was opened by the Austrian guard, that the fugitives might escape from the place. The insolent officer of the guard abused us for *Lutheran dogs*, and with this appellation gave a blow to each as he passed through the gate." In the most forlorn condition, without a single shilling in his possession, and with nothing but the clothes he wore, Heyne hastened to Aensdorf, a neighbouring town, where he was received for a few days by some acquaintance; from whence, after a time, he ventured back to Dresden, where he took up his quarters in Count Bruhl's empty library.

To add to all these personal sorrows, his beloved Theresa was taken dangerously ill; and having lost all her property in the conflagration of the capital, she was left entirely destitute. Her situation was as melancholy as his own; for she was completely cut off from her family, and without a home. Under these calamitous circumstances the lovers took the desperate resolution of sharing each other's fate, and they were accordingly married at Aensdorf, in the month of June 1761.

Heyne has related, with the utmost frankness and simplicity, the subsequent history of his course. After his marriage his prospects gradually brightened. Some mutual friends of the young couple interested themselves to procure him an employment in Lusatia, in a worthy family named Leoben, with whom he passed some years in complete seclusion, occupied in managing the estates of his patron, and "acquiring some notions of rural economy," his literary labours being almost wholly laid aside.

At length peace returned, and Heyne removed with his family to Dresden, where he learned that inquiries had been made concerning him from Hanover. He had no idea of the cause of these inquiries; but in the December following he was invited to accept the professorship at Gottingen, vacant by the death of Gesner. "I wrote," he tells us, " frankly to the prime minister, Von Münchausen, that I had got out of the track of all my studies, but hoped soon to be able to find my way into it again; and that if he would accept me after this acknowledgment, I was ready to accept his offer. On the 4th February 1763 I received the appointment, and arrived at Gottingen in the following June."

This appointment effectually secured him from all future anxiety as to pecuniary matters. He held it for the remainder of his life—a period of nearly fifty years. The manner in which he was introduced to the notice of the minister deserves to be related. The vacant situation was first offered to Professor Ruhnken, of Leyden, who declined to accept it, and in his reply thus expressed himself:—"Why seek out of the country what the country is so capable of furnishing? Why not give to Gesner for a successor Christian Gottlob Heyne, a man of extraordinary genius, who has proved his profound knowledge of Roman literature by his Tibullus, and of Greek by his Epictetus? In the opinion of myself, and of the great Hemsterhuis, he is the only one that can supply Gesner's place. Believe me, in this man there is such an exuberance of genius and learning, that all civilized Europe will soon resound with his praise." Thus sagaciously prophesied Ruhnken, and the result abundantly justified his words.

As a matter of course, Heyne, in his new situation, devoted himself to authorship. His successive publications, and the attraction of his lectures, placed him, in due time, among the most celebrated scholars of his age. He was, indeed, precisely in the situation best adapted to the exercise of his talents; and, blessed with domestic happiness, he thankfully acknowledged the goodness of God in thus securing to him what, at one period of his life, appeared hopelessly beyond his reach.

In the year 1775 he lost his excellent wife, who, by her prudence and affection, had made herself the joy and comfort of his life amidst years of solitude and sorrow. Under this most heavy trial Heyne had recourse to the consolations of religion. He was accustomed, in times of severe calamity, to commit to writing his reasons for consolation; and this he did on the present occasion. He commenced his reflections with the assurance, "Whatever befalls me is the work of a wise and beneficent Being who directs everything to the best ends;" and he concluded them with this exclamation, "Thanks be unto thee, then, O my God, for all sufferings and trials!"

Left with a young family, and burdened with the weighty duties of his important avocations, he found it desirable to marry a second time. His choice was a happy one; and, both in his private and public career, he prospered greatly. Whilst he was beloved and venerated in his own family and by his pupils, he was esteemed and honoured by all ranks of his fellow-citizens, who felt that he was an honour to their city, and the chief ornament of their university.

His son-in-law, who was his biographer, dwells much on his ardent charity. He had suffered so much that he knew the heart of a sufferer, and he was always devising means for succouring the unfortunate. Often he gave beyond his means; always he enjoined silence upon the objects of his bounty. His temperament was ardent and vivacious, but not devoid of delicacy and tender sensibility. Those who knew him most intimately, loved him and admired him most. He died on the 14th July 1812, at the age of eighty-two years and nine months. At the time of his death he was a member of most of the literary and philosophical societies in Europe, including the Royal and Antiquarian Societies of London.

John Bacon.

THIS celebrated artist, who was one of the earliest exhibitors in the Royal Academy, and the first who received the gold medal as a modeller in that institution, was born at Southwark, in Surrey, on the 24th November 1740. His father, Thomas Bacon, was a cloth-worker, who had left his native county in early life, and sought fortune in London, but with so little success that, when John was very young, he was obliged to work along with him for the maintenance of the family. His life was twice endangered in childhood. When about five years old, he fell into the pit of a soap-boiler, and must have perished, had not a man accidentally caught a sight of his head. A month after, he fell under a loaded cart, and escaped only by a surprising accident. His education was necessarily very limited, as his parents could not afford to pay for his schooling; but while he was a mere boy, he showed some symptoms of his future genius, discovering an early love for pictures and figures, and even attempting to draw. Though employed about work of the humblest kind, his young mind already felt the stirrings of ambition, and he longed for some worthier pursuit. "Even at this age," says his biographer, "he conceived that happiness was in every man's power who could learn to discipline his own mind; and on this plan he made a sort of philosophical attempt to command his own happiness."

It is not known at what time or by what means Bacon received his first religious impressions, but it is probable he imbibed them when a youth. His ancestors were pious people, and his father was remarkable for his devoutness, and seldom sat down to a meal without opening his Bible. The instructions and example of this good man, it can scarcely be doubted, influenced the mind of his son, and it is a matter of known experience that the children of truly Christian parents often receive deeper convictions in early years than is known or expressed at the time. The seed lies hidden, but it is not lost; and truly there is something forcibly impressive in the life of a good man. It silently, yet often irresistibly, affects the heart. Our artist, when arrived at the age of manhood, proved himself a true and devoted Christian, and for many years before his death, was a bright example to his family and those around him.

At the age of fourteen, Bacon was apprenticed to a Mr. Crispe of Bow Church-yard, an eminent maker of porcelain, who taught him the art of modelling shepherds and shepherdesses, and such small ornamental pieces as are commonly made for use or show at these works. This was the first step in the direction of his future art, and so great were his industry and skill, that in less than two years he made all the models for the manufactory, and his earnings were so considerable as to be the principal support of his parents. The dutiful lad, we are told, gladly abridged himself even of the necessaries of life in order to render this assistance as great as possible.

It was an accident which first awakened in his mind a strong inclination for his future profession. While attending the manufactory at Lambeth, he had an opportunity of observing the models of different sculptors, who sent them to be burnt at a pottery on the same premises. These he examined with curiosity and delight, and soon the desire arose within him to imitate works which he perceived were incomparably superior to the groups and figures manufactured by his master. The sight of these treasures stimulated his ambition, and he spent all his leisure hours in efforts to model in the same style. In short, he thus disciplined his hand and eye in the wisest manner, and at the same time, with the utmost prudence, he continued to work at his business, which furnished him with the means of independence, and, dearer still, the means of supplying his parents' necessities. At length, at the age of nineteen, when still an unknown labourer in Crispe's shop, he ventured to present the first of his productions, which he judged worthy of notice, to the Academy of Arts. This, which was called merely "A model in clay," received a premium of ten guineas. With the most praiseworthy industry, Bacon produced eight other works, for which prizes were adjudged to him to the amount of more than £200. So great was his unremitting application to his beloved art, even from the first commencement of his career.

How long Bacon continued at the pottery we are not told; but it was during his apprenticeship he first formed the idea of making statues in artificial stone. The invention was of earlier date, but to him was due the credit of having rendered it popular. He soon obtained occupation in this line at Mrs. Coade's artificial stone manufactory, established in 1769, and by his talents greatly assisted to advance the interests of the establishment, speaking of which Nichols, in his "History of Lambeth," says, "Here are many statues, which are allowed by the best judges to be master-pieces of art, from the models of that celebrated artist, John Bacon, Esq."

In 1763, he first attempted working in marble. He then lived in George Yard, near Soho Square, and exhibited a medallion of King George III., and a group of Bacchanalians. In the succeeding year he produced a model in bas-relief, the subject being the good Samaritan. His name was now gradually becoming known, and commissions of various kinds were entrusted to his skill. It became desirable that he should remove to a more convenient situation. "Accordingly, he took," says one of his biographers, "a little shop and lodgings in Wardour Street, where, in a studio half above ground, and half below, he commenced his contest for bread and fame, and he was soon master of both." When in his twenty-eighth year he entered the Royal Academy as a student, and there first received instruction in his profession, having never before seen the art of modelling or sculpture regularly executed by men of science. In 1769, he had the high honour of receiving the first gold medal for sculpture ever given by the Royal Academy. Two years after, he exhibited a cast from his model of Mars—a very beautiful performance, of which he afterwards carved in marble a statue as large as life. This work obtained for the sculptor the notice of the Archbishop of York, who introduced him to the royal patronage, and the king himself sat to Bacon for his bust. The following story is told of the statue of Mars:— Whilst the artist was making the model, so imperfectly was the clay wrought together that the figure shrunk down, and the nether limbs were crushed out of proportion. A porter came into his study with a letter, and, never having seen a human figure in clay before, could not conceal his wonder. "What a fine fellow," he said, "and with such short thighs, too!" The sculptor looked at his work, saw what had hap-

THE KING SITTING FOR HIS BUST.

pened, and repaired the accident, of which he had been so unceremoniously admonished.

The skill which Bacon showed in the royal bust, and his modest and unassuming bearing much pleased the king, who inquired if he had learned his art abroad, and whether he had studied at Rome. Being answered that he had never been out of the kingdom, the monarch said, "I am glad of it; you will be the greater honour to it." Having now secured to himself a fair prospect of future success, he married a lady to whom he had long been attached, and removed to Newman Street, where he had studios, shops, and everything desirable for carrying on his profession on a large scale. He soon obtained as many commissions as he could execute. The city of London entrusted to him the execution of a monument to the Earl of Chatham for the Guild-hall. When it was erected, we are told, "half the people of London flocked to see a work which the prints of the day declared to be 'most magnificent.'" In 1778, he commenced the monument of the same illustrious man in Westminster Abbey. It was completed in 1783. Of this work, and a monument for Mrs. Withers, these lines by Cowper are commemorative:—

> Bacon there
> Gives more than female beauty to a stone,
> And Chatham's eloquence to marble lips;
> Nor does the chisel occupy alone
> The powers of sculpture, but the style as much.

One day, while he was in Westminster Abbey, the artist was addressed by a stranger, who said, pointing to his monument to Chatham, "It is admirable, sir, upon the whole; but it has great defects." "I should feel obliged," said the sculptor, "if you would be so kind as to point them out to me." "Gladly!" replied the stranger. "Why here! and there! and there;—don't you see? Bad, very bad;" and at every word he spoke he struck the places alluded to with the iron end of his walking staff, in a manner that seemed like to injure the work. "But will you tell me, sir," said Bacon, "your reason for thinking those parts bad?" "I have already done so to the artist himself," said the critic, "so I shall not repeat them to you. I pointed out other defects, too, while the monument was forming, but he refused to be convinced." "Do you say you are personally acquainted with Bacon?" demanded the astonished sculptor. "Oh, yes, sir," replied the other; "I have been intimate with him for many years; a clever man, sir, but obstinate." "Were Bacon here now," said the artist, turning away, "he would not like to hear a *friend* of such old standing speaking of his work so roughly."

Another anecdote is related with reference to the same statue. While Bacon was re-touching it, a clergyman, a stranger, tapped him on the shoulder, and said, in allusion to a classical story, "Take care what you are doing; you work for eternity." The next day this reverend individual stept into the pulpit and preached. When the sermon was over, Bacon, who was of the audience, touched his arm, and said, "Take care what you do; *you* work for eternity."

Many other marble statues were executed by Bacon. His skill in carving the marble continually increased, so much so that it is said in every succeeding statue there was a visible improvement. "The flesh became more flexible, and the draperies more flowing. The artist seems to have been conscious wherein his strength lay. "I cannot grasp," he once said, "much less arrange at one time, several ideas. If I have anything distinguishing it as a knack at expressing an idea single and detached, I stick to my mistress—*Nature*—and she often lends me her hand." One of his sons said, "he used continually to inculcate the importance of a man's attending to that one point in which he discovered his chief talent to lie, and mentioned himself as an instance of the success attending this principle." What admirable good sense is there in this observation. It has been said of Bacon by an excellent critic, "He infused more good English sense into his sculpture than any preceding artist;" and this sterling quality, in whatever direction it is exercised, never fails to command confidence and secure success. Doubtless, this it was which in no small degree contributed to render him so popular. In 1780—but a few years from the time when he was an untaught and obscure workman in Coade's establishment—his reputation had spread far and wide through the land. His works were seen in Cathedrals, collections, and galleries, he had become a distinguished member of the Royal Academy, and associated with men of wealth and station. Lucrative commissions poured in upon him, and he was steadily progressing upward. So rapid and surprising a rise would have unhinged a man of weak mind, and rendered him vain and self-opinionated; but Bacon's friends found him ever disposed to entertain a humble opinion of his own merits, while, as a Christian, he constantly referred to his entire dependence on the divine aid, and dwelt on the folly and sin of pride. "We are (he would say) all beggars at the best; but we are apt to forget it, and that is one source of our pride. Two beggars stand at a door; one receives a penny, the other a guinea. It is well if the latter does not begin to imagine reason for the distinction, well if he does not swell upon it, and turn in contempt upon his fellow. Yet this is but a picture of a man's admiration of his gifts." These sentiments made Bacon fearful of his success, rendered him self-diffident, and caused him to set a guard upon his feelings, and to receive thankfully the admonitions of his friends. Of his occupation he said on one occasion, "I consider the profession in which I am providentially placed, and have honourably succeeded, as perfectly lawful, and that the monumental part of it may be employed to an important moral purpose."

In his private character Bacon was deservedly esteemed as a consistent Christian, and an excellent father and master. He employed all the means in his power to induce his children to follow his example, and that they might be guarded from the temptations of an alluring world, he sought to make their home a happy and attractive one. He was not only a pious father, but a pleasant friend and companion to them, and his affectionate disposition particularly endeared him to the little ones. He was equally skilful in instructing and in entertaining them. He would take some story from the Bible, and telling it in a simple, novel, and lively manner, would secure the child's interest, and fix the facts upon its memory. So warm and lively were his feelings and sympathies that they often expressed themselves in tears; his kind heart prompted him to deeds of kindness, and he even used to watch his workmen in times of sickness, and talk to them on the great subject that lay nearest to his heart. Occasionally he would pray with them at their bedside. Occupied with business, held in high repute and favour, and tempted with wealth, religion was still his great concern. He loved and sacredly observed the Sabbath-day, nor would he, on any consideration, attend to his worldly affairs during those sacred hours.

In many ways he evinced his conscientious and earnest desire to do good. He wrote numerous epitaphs, which he hoped might catch the eye of the stranger wandering in a churchyard, and produce a beneficial impression on the heart. With the same object he composed a great number of fables for the instruction of the ignorant and the inculcation of moral and religious principles. Shortly before his death, he was greatly interested in the formation of a literary society, whose object it should be to oppose works of an irreligious and infidel tendency, and the same zeal in a good cause made him ever ready to assist in religious and charitable designs.

Bacon may be regarded as an illustration of that Scriptural axiom, "Godliness is profitable for all things, having promise of the life that now is, and of that which is to come." His earnest piety and strict integrity were no impediments in his way to fortune. On the contrary, they assisted to help him on. To whatever subject he applied himself, his affairs prospered; and it cannot be doubted that his high-toned morality and exemplary conduct served to advance his worldly interests. There were not wanting, indeed, those who, envious of his prosperity, and misunderstanding the true character of the man, were disposed to impute to him unworthy motives, supposing his piety and zeal to be ostentatious, and from interested motives; but they who knew him best bore ample testimony to his true worth and heartfelt sincerity.

Amidst all his diversified occupations in public and in private, the artist continued his professional labours with undiminished ardour, and with equal success, to the close of his life. He lived fifty-eight years. Every succeeding year had added to his fame, and brought an increase of employment. His health appeared vigorous, and his frame strong, and it might have been anticipated that his life would be extended to an advanced period; but by a sudden attack of inflammation, his strength was exhausted in little more than two days, and he sank into the arms of death, expiring on the 7th August 1799.

Thus departed a man who, while successful beyond all expectation in the affairs of this life, had wisdom and grace to use without abusing his good fortune; and instead of taking this world as his portion, aspired to the higher honours and unfading rewards of eternity. He was decided on the great point, and having made his choice determinately pursued it. Happy he! happy all who, like him, walking by faith, have "respect to the recompence of the reward."

Bacon was buried in Whitfield's chapel, Tottenham Court-Road, and a plain tablet was placed over his grave for which he had written the following inscription:—

"WHAT I WAS AS AN ARTIST, SEEMED TO ME OF SOME IMPORTANCE WHILE I LIVED;
BUT WHAT I REALLY WAS AS A BELIEVER IN CHRIST JESUS,
IS THE ONLY THING OF IMPORTANCE TO ME NOW.

Louis Holberg.

FEW names are held in higher repute among the Danes than that of Louis, Baron Holberg, who is justly regarded by them as the founder of their modern school of literature. He devoted his whole life to study, and acquired in his own country distinguished renown as a satirist, a dramatic writer, and a national historian, as well as an expounder of the principles of public law.

Far from inheriting a title or patrimony, this extraordinary man was of obscure family—his father having been originally a common soldier, who rose from the ranks to the command of a regiment, having maintained through life the character of a just, brave, and pious man. The events of Holberg's life have been related by himself in a series of letters, published in the Latin language, about the year 1737; a vein of good sense and humour enlivens the narration, and the whole is evidently a correct picture of the writer and his adventures. The death of his father, which occurred when he was an infant, left the family in very straitened circumstances, and it was only by the strictest economy that the widow contrived to make the pittance she was mistress of suffice for the wants of her children. The worthy woman died when her son Louis was ten years old; and, as it was at that time the practice in Norway to give pay to the children of officers, and to initiate them almost from the cradle in military tactics, the child was placed at a military school at Upland; but having, even at that early age, given decided indications of a passion for literature, one of his relatives, to whose care he was intrusted, placed him under the tuition of a private master. This man was brutal and ignorant, and never suffered a day to pass without flogging his pupils. "If I had not," says Holberg, "fallen into the hands of this tyrant, I might have boasted that, during the whole period of my pupilage, I had never once been flogged; for I was a great favourite with my other masters, public as well as private. I remember, on one occasion, when the usher of the second class in the public school at Bergen gave me a slight stroke on the hand with a cane, I was so indignant at receiving this punishment that I turned fiercely upon him, and called him an old goat—a name by which the boys distinguished him from the other ushers, on account of the length of his beard. The good man bore this affront with dignified indifference, simply contenting himself with calling me a little blockhead, though, if any other boy had dared to use such language, his resentment would certainly not have been confined within such moderate limits."

From the grammar school of Bergen the lad was sent to the university of Copenhagen, his scholastic studies having been cut short, partly because the school at Bergen was reduced to ashes by the great fire which occurred in that town in 1702, and partly because the master of the school considered him not much inferior in point of scholarship to those who were of an age to be dismissed. His pecuniary circumstances did not permit him to stay long at Copenhagen; and when he had passed his examination, he returned to Norway, and shortly after became tutor to the children of a country clergyman, who stipulated that, whenever he should be prevented by illness, or any other cause, from discharging his theological functions, the youthful mentor should take his place, and expound the doctrines of the Christian religion to the rustics. With characteristic humour, he describes himself as passing a year in flogging his pupils and converting Norwegian boors. "I had better success," says he, "as a preacher than as a pedagogue; for I was dismissed without much ceremony for too vigorous an exercise of the birch on the youngest son of my master, who was an unimprovable dunce and his mother's darling; but, on the other hand, I received, on my departure, the most flattering testimonies of approbation from the rustics, who did not hesitate to compare me to the late preacher, Peter, whose eloquence was in that country considered equal to that of Chrysostom. I did not regret my dismissal, for the task of teaching is especially irksome to a man of irritable temper. . . . I proceeded again to Copenhagen, in order to pass a final examination; and, during my residence in the university, received some instruction in the French and Italian languages, not neglecting, however, my sacred studies, in which I made such proficiency, that, at the end of the winter, I obtained a high theological degree, and returned home with a good character, but an empty purse."

Under these circumstances, the unfortunate student had no resource but to accept a fresh tutorship in the family of Nicholas Schmidt, the vice-bishop of Bergen. This new patron had, in his younger days, travelled over several countries of Europe, and he had kept a journal of his travels, which Holberg eagerly read in his leisure hours, and imbibed from its perusal an ardent desire to visit foreign lands. His poverty appeared, indeed, an insurmountable obstacle to the gratification of his desires; but, quitting his situation, in which he speedily began "to feel like a man condemned to the mines," he proceeded to turn "everything he could collect—goods, chattels, and hereditaments"—into money. Small was the sum total thus obtained; but, firm to his purpose, he embarked for Holland—feeling confident that, when his cash was exhausted, he should be able to maintain himself by teaching the French and Italian languages.

Arrived at Amsterdam, he soon discovered that that city would not be favourable to his purposes—"literary acquirements being quite at a discount where trade occupied every man's thoughts." In this dilemma, which was rendered the more embarrassing by a threatening attack of fever, he repaired to Aix la Chapelle, with but six imperials in his purse, and a passport for which he had paid dear, but which he could not read without indignation, for it appeared to him rather a satire than a testimonial. The document was couched in these terms:—" Laissez passer et repasser le garçon Louis d'Holberg d'Amsterdam." His extremely youthful appearance had exposed him to derision on more than one occasion; for he had heard some of his fellow travellers observe that he ought to be examined, and made to explain how it happened that he had left Norway alone, at an age when boys who cannot swim without corks (as the proverb says) seldom venture to travel beyond the limits of their native country. On one occasion, he relates that a certain priest approached him with a magisterial air, and asked him when he had run away from school? "So great was my indignation at this insult," he says, "that, before the man could add another word, I poured forth a volley of Latin phrases, which completely astonished and confounded my defenceless adversary, who finding it expedient to abandon his dictatorial tone, exclaimed, with respectful humility, 'The gentleman is a theologian! I congratulate you, sir.'"

At the end of three weeks, spent at Aix la Chapelle, his finances were completely exhausted, and he had recourse to an expedient which, he assures us, neither before nor after, ever entered his mind—that of sneaking off without paying his bill. "Having packed up my clothes in my portmanteau, I rose at daybreak, and crept out at a back-door. But I was a very inexperienced cheat; and my host, who suspected my intentions, was on the watch for me, seized me at the threshold, and compelled me to satisfy his demands. This scene made a deep impression upon me; for a long time the image of my host was perpetually before my eyes; even in my dreams I saw him fastening upon my throat, and dragging me back with reproaches, which I had but too well merited, to the inn."

The payment of this bill having left him moneyless, he was compelled to return on foot to Holland. With great difficulty he procured sufficient money at Amsterdam to pay his expenses to Norway. For some time he was in doubt whether he should return to Bergen or to Christiansand. At length he decided in favour of the latter place, where he formed acquaintance with a student of Drontheim, named Christian Brixius, by whom he was recommended to several of the principal inhabitants, whose children he instructed in the French and other foreign languages. After some weeks he received an invitation from a clergyman, who was distantly related to him, and in whose house he spent the winter, and in return taught the children of the family the elements of the English language. He modestly says—" A superficial knowledge of three or four languages had obtained for me a great reputation among the inhabitants of Christiansand; and I well remember, when I was sauntering one day through the town, being followed by two young men, one of whom observed to the other, 'That is the great scholar who knows so many languages, and speaks French, Italian, Polish, Russian, and Turkish.' I was as distinguished a person in Christiansand as Mithridates, king of Pontus, was in Asia; and everybody knows that historians record of that monarch that he could speak twenty-two languages."

Having saved a small sum by his exertions in teaching, Holberg now determined to visit England, and his friend Brixius agreed to accompany him. The two companions arrived at Gravesend, and proceeded on foot to London—Holberg acting as interpreter for Brixius, who was ignorant of the English language. They stayed a short time in the metropolis, and then proceeded to Oxford; where, though their finances were at a low ebb, they spent some crowns in obtaining access to the libraries. Their eagerness in examining and collating manuscripts was checked by the necessity of supplying their daily wants. "My companion," says Holberg, "professed music, and I grammar; but, as we were no great proficients in the sciences we professed, we could not turn our acquisitions to much account in a place where it was to be expected that sound knowledge could alone insure the success of a teacher. We lived three months at Oxford with so rigid an attention to economy, that we ate meat only once in four days; on the other three we were obliged to be contented with bread and cheese, or even a more scanty and unsubstantial repast."

This frugal mode of living agreed very well with Holberg, who had long been accustomed to it; but it was otherwise with Brixius, who, after a time, quitted Oxford, leaving his friend to pursue his studies alone. This departure for a time annoyed him, but he soon found consolation in the intimacy he formed with the students of the university. Many of these took every opportunity of eulogizing his learning and good qualities; his knowledge of foreign languages, and his skill in music, attracted much admiration, and procured him a host of pupils. Holberg was not ungrateful to the Oxonians; he thus praises their kind-heartedness and generosity:—" I remained at Oxford, after the departure of Brixius, about fifteen months, during all which time I lived in a gay and sumptuous style—being invited almost every day by the fellows of colleges to dine and sup, or, as they say at Oxford, to take commons with them. . . . I have many reasons for considering myself under great obligations to the Oxonians, and I cannot omit mentioning one among many other proofs of their kindness and liberality towards me. After sojourning nearly two years at Oxford, when I had determined to return to my native country, a fellow of Magdalen College called me aside, and begged me to declare candidly the state of my finances; adding, that the whole college would raise a liberal supply for me, if my scruples in point of delicacy could be overcome. My gratitude for this kind and liberal offer was unbounded; but as I was not destitute of the means of defraying my expenses, I magnanimously declined it; so that the reader may divide his admiration between the generosity of the man who made the offer, and the sturdy independence of the man who refused it. I am deeply sensible of the various good offices which I received from the Oxonians. I never cringed to any man; servility and obsequiousness being foreign to my nature. I knew these gentlemen respected me for my correct and moral deportment, and they were pleased with the sprightliness of my conversation: this being a quality in which the English much delight, especially if it be seasoned with humour, in which they are themselves far from deficient."

Holberg at length left Oxford; and, after a short sojourn in London, he embarked on board a Swedish vessel, and landed safely at Elsinore, from whence he proceeded, on foot, to Copenhagen, where he again accepted a situation as tutor to the son of a counsellor of state, and with his pupil he travelled through Germany, where the pedantry of the professors called forth the sallies of his wit and ridicule. On his return from this, his third, expedition, he was admitted a member of the Medicean College. During his residence of two years in that college he published two works. The first was an Introduction to European History. It appears he had commenced it in England, where, he tells us, he consulted the books from which the materials were taken, in the Bodleian Library, and where he was "animated with the desire of becoming an author before he had acquired a beard." This work was speedily followed by another on Universal History; and, shortly after, he undertook an Introduction to the History of Denmark, which procured him the appointment of Historical Professor. The emoluments of this office being very small, Holberg obtained a temporary pension, subject to the liability of being sent abroad to the Protestant academies. He was selected for foreign service, and he gladly availed himself of the opportunity for travelling, and made his way to Paris, where he passed the years 1714 and 1715. In the morning he frequented the libraries; in the evening, the theatres. He studied men and manners with keen and observant eye, disputed with the theologians of St. Sulpice, and with the wits of the Café Marion, and frequently attended the Palace of Justice, to observe the way in which the French civil law was administered. In the meantime, he attained proficiency in the French language, and made himself well acquainted with the genius of its comedians and satirists—Montaigne, Scarron, Boileau, and Moliére being his favourite authors. Despite the meagreness of his resources, he next determined on a journey to Italy; for, says he, "the passion for travelling grows stronger; and he who is once seized with it can no more stop short, than the despairing lover who has precipitated himself from the fatal rock."

This new journey was, for the most part, accomplished on foot; but, on one occasion, when sailing from Leghorn to Civita Vecchia, he narrowly escaped the same fate as befell the illustrious Cervantes—the ship in which he had taken passage being attacked by Algerine pirates. His description of the incident is exceedingly characteristic:—"One of the ships, called by the Italians *Conserva*, which protect merchant vessels, came to our assistance. The sailors were placed at the guns, the passengers were furnished with arms, and every preparation was made for the combat. I was awakened by the noise, and was seized with a fit of shivering, and quite expected a fresh attack of my recent quartan. The fit having subsided, I joined the terrified passengers, uttering no expression of alarm, except, perhaps, announcing my conviction that every soul on board would perish —a conviction which afforded me much consolation, for calamity is deprived of half its severity when it is shared with great numbers! The Italian women rushed from their cabin with dishevelled hair, and the vessel re-echoed with their screams and lamentations. The monks displayed as little firmness as the women. Some of them struck their heads with their fists; others, stretched on the ground, were invoking the aid of their favourite saints; nor could any entreaties or reproaches of the other passengers induce them to suspend these unmanly lamentations, and betake themselves to their own and the ship's defence. I must myself at this moment have presented a ludicrous spectacle: pale and emaciated as I was, I was placed, sword in hand, in order of battle, and in that position implored the aid of St. Anthony, in common with my fellow-passengers. But the pirates, neglecting us, attacked the other ship; and, while they were so engaged, we took the opportunity of making all the sail we could, and effected our escape. Delivered from this danger, we arrived at length at Civita Vecchia, where I determined to proceed to Rome on foot, thinking it a less evil than to contend with the tide of the Tiber for three successive days; but I found the whole road leading to the Eternal City so infested with serpents, that I scarcely ventured to repose on the ground during the entire journey."

Holberg lost no time in visiting the public libraries, where, however, he found his principal object completely thwarted, no one being permitted to read prohibited works without leave from the inquisitors; hence, like another Tantalus, he found himself starved in the midst of abundance, for almost every book he asked for belonged to the prohibited class. "My studies were consequently restricted within very narrow limits," he says, "being chiefly confined to Roman antiquities, and some modern descriptions of Rome, which served to guide me in my walks through the city and amid the monuments of former grandeur. . . . . . If, however, during my residence at Rome, I made little progress in polite studies, I, at any rate, gained some acquaintance with that important branch of science which one learns in the kitchen. I learned precisely how much time and fuel were requisite to make a soup and boil a cabbage, and how many Ave Marias were necessary to ensure the tossing up an omelet successfully; if, therefore, the culinary art be entitled to any respect, I did not visit Rome without acquiring something valuable. That my time might not be quite absorbed in these occupations, it was my wont to place pen and paper close by the fire-side, so that, while holding a book in one hand, I could stir my soup or porridge with the other. I learned thus, to my cost, that one cannot well play the cook and the philosopher at the same moment; for it frequently chanced that, while I was reading or writing too intently, my macaroni was burnt to a cinder, or my soup boiled over. At first I felt ashamed of this menial employment; but that feeling quickly subsided

HOLBERG AS COOK AND PHILOSOPHER.

when I perceived that there was nothing more common in Italy. In my hotel were two Neapolitan noblemen, whom I often caught engaged in the same manner; and when the doors of our respective chambers were left open, a sort of concert was kept up by our different frying-pans, in which mine, being the smaller pan, played the treble, and theirs the bass."

At the end of six months this lively and restless being determined to retrace his steps to his native land, and again walked almost the whole distance. After his return, he remained during two years, "struggling with the greatest difficulties," occasioned by the narrowness of his income. At the end of that time he was appointed Professor of Metaphysics; and in 1717 he obtained the situation of "Consistorial Assessor," a place of dignity and profit to which his standing in the university entitled him.

There was now an end of his troubles and his adventures. During the remainder of his life, as he informs us, his struggles were confined to a warfare against bad taste, pedants, and pretenders. He gave himself, with surprising diligence, to the composition of a host of works,—his pen being so prolific, that there is no department of literature which he left unattempted, with the exception of tragedy. History, biography, philosophy, and politics, all, in turns, engaged his attention. He gives in his narrative a detailed account of these various works, and states that it was not till he had attained his thirtieth year that he suddenly felt prompted to attempt poetry. His first effort was an imitation of Juvenal's Satires, followed by his "Peter Paars," which at once astonished and delighted his countrymen: "that celebrated heroic poem," says its author, "is now committed to memory even by Swedes and Germans, whom its popularity has induced to learn the Danish language." This production has acquired for Holberg the title of the Danish Butler. In its style it is lively and diverting,—its design being to satirize the vices and follies of the writer's contemporaries. According to Malte Brun, it resembles a gallery of Ostades and Teniers. Holberg's plays, amounting in all to nearly forty, are so admirable that a modern critic, who has studied the dramatic authors of all nations, pronounces him worthy to take place as a comic poet with Plautus and Molière. In a satirical poem entitled "Metamorphoses," our author reverses the system of Ovid,—animals being transformed into men, instead of men into animals. But that which has been perhaps the most renowned of his productions is "Klimm's Subterranean Journey," a philosophical satire, written originally in Latin, but translated not only into Danish, but into almost all the European languages.

It would be impossible to enumerate severally all the writings of Holberg. Among the most important are his "History of Denmark," his "Universal History," his "Ecclesiastical History," and his "History of the Jews." His select works alone amount to twenty-one octavo volumes. In his autobiography he enlists our sympathies by the naiveté with which he relates his feelings during the various periods of his career. He was always infirm in health, or, as he says, "frequently labouring under indisposition as well of mind as of body;" but in his literary pursuits he found consolation, and pronounces it to be his conviction that there is no calamity in this world which literature cannot in some measure contribute to alleviate. "I know not, indeed," he adds, "how I should have supported many of the troubles I have experienced in life if I had not taken refuge in the haven of philosophy. My studies have taken a wide range, embracing all subjects and sciences, except medicine and mathematics, which I did not understand."

It was while engaged in writing his political history of Denmark and Sweden that his labours were painfully interrupted by that calamitous and almost unprecedented occurrence, the great fire of Copenhagen. Holberg has given an impressive account of its horrors, and of the fearful losses suffered by the inhabitants:—"It was not till the ravages of the flames had ceased that men began to feel the full weight of the calamity, and the whole extent of their private losses. Some, whose wealth consisted chiefly of splendid personal possessions, were reduced at once from a state of affluence to abject poverty, and they who had lately kept splendid equipages were now seen among the meanest pedestrians, or compelled to solicit the charitable donations which they once generously bestowed. For my part, I regretted the change of residence entailed upon me by the fire much more than the loss of property I had sustained by it. I regretted the separation from my old friends, and the loss of my old study, where I had spent so many tranquil years among my books and papers; for to me nothing is more delightful than tranquillity, and a systematic regularity in my mode of living. With me everything was system; my business, my relaxation, my waking, my sleeping hours, my serious and my trifling pursuits, all were arranged and came round in regular succession. I spent some days in searching every corner of the part of the city saved from the flames, in order to find a convenient lodging; and I at last found a place in which, after making a few requisite arrangements, I was enabled in a short time to resume my former way of living."

Thus, in his cherished retirement, as years advanced, he continued, with unabated diligence, to prosecute his studies, and to publish their results. He depicts himself, after his own fashion, in a half-humorous manner, with income so much increased, that he was enabled to live in a more elegant style than formerly, yet still adhering to his old routine; rambling on foot about the town, and splashed with mud from the passing carriages, rather than ride; simple and inexpensive in his habits, devoting two or three hours every day to walking or the society of his friends, and dividing the remainder between his two great sources of enjoyment—literature and music. "Some of my well-wishers," he concludes, "attribute my way of living to avarice and penuriousness; but, in truth, I give yearly to the poor as much as I should pay an idle hireling to wait on me and spy upon my conduct. I live in a handsome house, dress like a gentleman, frequently buy books; and, to give a final answer to all injurious surmises, I have determined to devote all my money to the public service."

Although somewhat resembling the French in wit and manners, Holberg pronounces himself an admirer of the English character, and speaks with evident pleasure of the happy government of the British nation; of their fertile soil, and of the various blessings which providence has lavished upon them. To sum up all, he pronounces the men for the more part brave, and the women beautiful: "The former have gained an ascendency abroad, but the latter reign paramount at home; for the English, who aim at universal dominion, patiently submit to the yoke of female government; and while they meet external aggression like lions, they cower under domestic tyranny like mice!" This last statement savours undoubtedly of the writer's characteristic penchant to satirize even what most he admires. He adds that, for his own part, the society of women had always pleased him better than that of men: their conversation he found more piquant and natural, and their abstemious habits and soothing manners better adapted to his peculiar tastes and predilections. Nevertheless, he remained unmarried; and at his death bequeathed the bulk of his property, which was considerable, to the Academy of Soroe, an institute founded with the patriotic object of preventing the Danish nobility from studying at foreign universities. He also settled a handsome sum, of which the interest was appropriated to provide establishments for poor and honest maidens at Copenhagen.

Frederick V. conferred the rank of nobility upon Holberg; and the honour was certainly well bestowed on the man who was the brighest ornament of that monarch's reign, and the creator of a national literature. Holberg's death occurred early in 1754: he had just attained his seventieth year.

William Gifford.

PERCHANCE among the readers of these annals there may be some youth who, though poor, forlorn, and ignorant, feels within him a thirst for knowledge, and is ready to undergo all labour and self-denial necessary for its attainment;—to such an one the example of this distinguished scholar and critic is presented, as well calculated to encourage and stimulate him. Among the many who have nobly surmounted the impediments thrown in the way of their intellectual progress, by humble birth and early indigence, William Gifford is assuredly one of the most remarkable. His biography has been traced by his own hand in so captivating and masterly a style that it would be unpardonable to mar it by any alterations, and it is therefore given here with some occasional abbreviations :—

"I know but little of my family, and that little is not very precise. My great-grandfather possessed considerable property at Kalsbury, a parish in the neighbourhood of Ashburton, but whether acquired or inherited I do not know. My grandfather was extravagant and dissipated. My father never mentioned his name; but my mother would sometimes tell me that he had ruined the family. My father was, as I have heard, 'a very wild young man, who could be kept to nothing.' He was sent to the grammar school at Exeter, from which he made his escape, and entered on board a man-of-war. He was reclaimed from this situation, and left his school a second time to wander in some vagabond society. On his return from this notable adventure, he was reduced to article himself to a plumber and glazier, with whom he luckily stayed long enough to learn the business. I suppose his father was now dead; for he became possessed of two small estates, married my mother—the daughter of a carpenter at Ashburton—and set up for himself with some credit at South Molton; but, after a residence there of four or five years, he thoughtlessly engaged in a dangerous frolic, which drove him once more to sea.

"My father was a good seaman, and was soon made second in command in the *Lyon*, a large armed transport in the service of Government, while my mother returned to her native place, Ashburton, where I was born, in April 1756.

"The resources of my mother were very scanty; she, however, did what she could for me, and, as soon as I was old enough to be trusted out of her sight, sent me to a schoolmistress of the name of Parret, from whom I learned in due time to read. I cannot boast much of my acquisitions at this school,—they consisted merely of the contents of the 'Child's Spelling Book,'—but from my mother, who had stored up the literature of a country town, which, about half a century ago, amounted to little more than what was disseminated by itinerant ballad-singers, or rather readers, I had acquired much curious knowledge of the Catskin, and the Golden Bull, and the Bloody Gardener, and many other histories equally instructive and amusing.

"My father returned from sea in 1764: he had been present at the siege of Havannah; and though he received more than a hundred pounds for prize-money, and his wages were considerable, yet, as he had not acquired any strict habits of economy, he brought home but a trifling sum. The little property yet left was therefore turned into money, and with this he set up a second time as a glazier and house-painter. I was now about eight years old, and was put to the free school, to learn to read, write, and cipher. Here I continued about three years, making most wretched progress, when my father fell sick and died; and in somewhat less than a twelvemonth my poor mother followed him to the grave. She was an excellent woman; bore her husband's infirmities with patience and good humour, loved her children dearly, and died at last, exhausted with anxiety and grief, more on their account than her own. I was not quite thirteen when this happened, my little brother was hardly two, and we had not a relation nor a friend in the world. Everything that was left was seized by a person of the name of Carlile, for money advanced to my mother. It may be supposed that I could not dispute the justice of his claims; and as no one else interfered, he was suffered to do as he liked. My little brother was sent to the alms-house, whither his nurse followed him out of pure affection, and I was taken to the house of Carlile, who was also my godfather. Respect for the opinion of the town induced him to send me again to school, where I was more diligent than before, and more successful. I grew fond of arithmetic, and my master began to distinguish me; but these golden days were over in less than three months. Carlile sickened at the expense, and looked round for an opportunity of ridding himself of a useless charge. He had previously attempted to engage me in the drudgery of husbandry. I drove the plough for one day to gratify him; but I left it with a firm resolution to do so no more. In this I was guided no less by necessity than will. I had never recovered the effects of a blow I had received in attempting to clamber up a table, and was made extremely sensible of them on any extraordinary exertion. Ploughing, therefore, was out of the question, and, as I have said, I utterly refused to follow it.

" As I could write and cipher (as the phrase is), Carlile next thought of sending me to Newfoundland, to assist in a storehouse. For this purpose he negotiated with a Mr. Holdsworthy of Dartmouth, who agreed to fit me out. But, on seeing me, this great man observed, with a look of pity and contempt, that I was 'too small,' and sent me away sufficiently mortified.

"My godfather had now humbler views for me, and I had little heart to resist anything. He proposed to send me on board one of the Torbay fishing boats; I ventured, however, to remonstrate against this, and the matter was compromised by my consenting to go on board a coaster. A coaster was speedily found for me at Brixham, and thither I went when little more than thirteen.

"My master, whose name was Full, though a gross and ignorant, was not an ill-natured man; at least not to me; and my mistress used me with unvarying kindness, moved perhaps by my weakness and tender years. In return, I did what I could to requite her, and my good will was not overlooked.

"Our vessel was not very large, nor our crew very numerous. On ordinary occasions, such as short trips to Dartmouth, Plymouth, &c., it consisted only of my master, an apprentice nearly out of his time, and myself: when we had to go further—to Portsmouth, for example—an additional hand was hired for the voyage. In this vessel I continued nearly a twelvemonth; and here got acquainted with nautical terms, and contracted a love for the sea, which a lapse of thirty years has little diminished.

"It will be easily conceived that my life was a life of hardship. I was not only a 'shipboy on the high and giddy mast,' but also in the cabin, where every menial office fell to my lot; yet if I was restless and discontented, I can safely say it was not so much on account of this, as of my being precluded from all possibility of reading; as my master did not possess, nor do I recollect seeing, during the whole time of my abode with him, a single book of any description, except the 'Coasting Pilot.'"

Out of this miserable condition the forlorn and friendless lad was rescued by an unexpected incident. The poor women at Brixham, who travelled to Ashburton with their fish twice a week, and who had known Gifford's parents, commiserated the boy when they saw him running about the beach with a ragged jacket and trousers, and carried the report of his melancholy change of condition to the people of Ashburton, whose pity was awakened by these tales; and there arose in consequence a general feeling of resentment against the man who had reduced him to such a state of wretchedness. The murmurs thus raised induced Carlile to recall his neglected charge, and to replace him at school.

"All this," he says, "I learned on my return, and my heart, which had been cruelly shut up, now opened to kinder sentiments and fairer views.

"I returned to my darling pursuit, arithmetic; my progress was so rapid that in a few months I was at the head of the school, and qualified to assist my master on any extraordinary emergency. As he usually gave me a trifle on these occasions, it raised a thought in me, that by engaging with him as a regular assistant, I might, with a little additional aid, be enabled to support myself. On mentioning my little plan to Carlile, he treated it with the utmost contempt, and told me that, as I had learned enough, and more than enough, at school, he must be considered as having fairly discharged his duty; he added that he had been negotiating with his cousin, a shoemaker of some respectability, who had liberally agreed to take me without a fee, as an apprentice. I was so shocked at this intelligence that I did not remonstrate, but went in sullenness and silence to my new master, to whom I was soon after bound, till I should attain the age of twenty-one. My indenture was dated 1st January 1772."

The family into which he was thus introduced consisted of four journeymen, two sons about his own age, and an apprentice somewhat older. In these there was nothing remarkable; but the master himself was a strange being, delighting in controversy, and upholding a favourite theological system of his own by dint of noise and vehement assertion. With these weapons he contrived to silence his opponents, and became, in consequence, intolerably arrogant and conceited.

"With such a man," says Gifford, "I was not

likely to add much to my stock of knowledge, small as it was; and indeed, nothing could well be smaller. At this period I had read nothing but a black letter romance, called 'Parismus and Parismenus,' and a few loose magazines which my mother had brought from South Molton. With the Bible, indeed, I was well acquainted; it was the favourite study of my grandmother, and reading it frequently with her had impressed it on my mind: these then, with the 'Imitation of Thomas à Kempis,' which I used to read to my mother on her deathbed, constituted the whole of my literary acquisitions.

"As I hated my new profession with a perfect hatred, I made no progress in it, and was, consequently, little regarded in the family, of which I sunk by degrees into the common drudge: this did not much disquiet me, for my spirits were now humbled. I secretly prosecuted my favourite study at every interval of leisure: these were not very frequent, and when the use I made of them was found out, they were rendered still less so.

"I possessed at this time but one book in the world: it was a treatise on algebra, given to me by a young woman who had found it in a lodging house. I considered it as a treasure, but it was a treasure locked up, for it supposed the reader to be well acquainted with simple equation, and I knew nothing of the matter. My master's son had purchased Fenning's 'Introduction;' this was precisely what

GIFFORD RECEIVING A TREATISE ON ALGEBRA.

I wanted, but he carefully concealed it from me, and I was indebted to chance alone for stumbling upon his hiding place. I sat up for the greatest part of several nights successively, and before he suspected that his treatise was discovered, had completely mastered it. I could now enter upon my own, and that carried me pretty far into the science.

"This was not done without difficulty. I had not a farthing on earth, nor a friend to give me one: pen, ink, and paper were therefore as completely out of my reach as a crown and sceptre. There was indeed a resource; but the utmost caution and secresy were necessary in applying to it. I beat out pieces of leather as smooth as possible, and wrought my problems on them with a blunted awl; for the rest, my memory was tenacious, and I could multiply and divide by it to a great extent.

"Hitherto I had not so much as dreamed of poetry; indeed I scarcely knew it by name; and whatever may be said of the force of nature, I certainly never 'lisped in numbers.' I recollect the occasion of my first attempt. A person whose name escapes me, had undertaken to paint a sign for an alehouse: it was to have been a lion, but the unfortunate artist produced a dog. On this awkward affair one of my acquaintance wrote a copy of what we called verse. I liked it, but fancied that I could compose something more to the purpose. I made the experiment, and by the universal suffrage of my shopmates, I succeeded. Another occurrence as trifling as the former furnished me with a fresh subject, and thus I went on till I had got together about a dozen of them. Certainly nothing was ever so deplorable; such as they were, however, they were talked of in my little circle, and I was sometimes invited to repeat them even out of it.

"These repetitions were always attended with applause, and sometimes with favours more substantial: little collections were now and then made, and I have received sixpence in an evening. To one who had lived so long in absolute want of money such a resource seemed a Peruvian mine: I furnished myself by degrees with paper, &c., and what was of more importance, with books of geometry and of the higher branches of algebra, which I cautiously concealed. Poetry was even at this time no amusement of mine, and I had only recourse to it when I wanted money for my mathematical pursuits.

"But the clouds were gathering fast. My master's anger was raised to a terrible pitch by my indifference to his concerns; and I was required to give up my papers. When I refused, my garret was searched, and my little hoard of books discovered and removed, and all future repetitions prohibited in the strictest manner.

"I look back on the part of my life which immediately followed with little satisfaction. It was a period of gloom and savage insociability. I crept on in silent discontent, unfriended and unpitied; indignant at the present, careless of the future, an object at once of apprehension and dislike.

"From this state of abjectness I was roused by a young woman of my own class. She was a neighbour, and whenever I took my solitary walk, with my 'Wolfius' in my pocket, she usually came to the door, and by a smile, or a short question, put in the friendliest manner, endeavoured to solicit my attention. My heart had long been shut to kindness, but the sentiment was not dead in me. It revived at the first encouraging word, and the gratitude I felt for it was the first pleasing sensation which I had ventured to entertain for many dreary months. I now strove by every winning art in my power to make my companions forget my former repulsive ways; nor was I unsuccessful; I recovered their good will, and by degrees grew to be somewhat of a favourite. My master still murmured, for the business of the shop went on no better than before: I comforted myself, however, with the reflection, that my apprenticeship was drawing to a conclusion, when I determined to renounce the employment for ever, and to open a private school.

" In this humble and obscure state, poor beyond the common lot, yet flattering my ambition with day-dreams which, perhaps, would never have been realized, I was found in the twentieth year of my age by Mr. William Cookesley, a name never to be pronounced by me without veneration. It was my good fortune to interest his benevolence. The lamentable doggerel which I have already mentioned had by some accident reached his ear, and given him a curiosity to inquire after the author.

" My little history was not without melancholy; and I laid it fairly before him; his first care was to console; his second, which he cherished to the last moment of his existence, was to relieve and support me.

"On examining into the nature of my literary attainments, he found them absolutely nothing; he heard, however, with equal surprise and pleasure, that, amidst the grossest ignorance of books, I had made a very considerable progress in the mathematics. He engaged me to enter into the details of this affair, and when he learned that I had made it under circumstances of peculiar discouragement, he became more warmly interested in my favour, as he now saw a possibility of serving me."

Through the kindness of this excellent friend—who was a surgeon, possessed of but limited means, but endowed with a generous and benevolent heart—a subscription was raised "for purchasing the remainder of the time of William Gifford, and for enabling him to improve himself in writing and English grammar." Sufficient was thus collected, in small sums, to free him from his apprenticeship, and to maintain him for a few months, during which he assiduously attended the free school. So great was the progress he made during that short period, and so favourable the report given of his diligence and talents, that it was determined by his patrons to renew their donations and continue him at school another year. This liberality was not lost upon Gifford, who, anxious to repay it to the utmost of his power, redoubled his diligence. He continues his narrative thus :—

"Now that I am sunk into indolence, I look back with some degree of scepticism to the exertions of that period. In two years and two months from the day of my emancipation I was pronounced by my master fit for the university. The plan of opening a writing school had been abandoned almost from the first, and Mr. Cookesley looked round for some one who had interest enough to procure me some little office at Oxford. This person, who was soon found, was Thomas Taylor, Esq., of Denbury, who procured me the place of Biblical Lecturer at Exeter College; and this, with such occasional assistance from the country as Mr. Cookesly undertook to provide, was thought sufficient to enable me to live, at least till I had taken a degree.

"During my attendance on Mr. Smerdon (my master), I had written several tuneful trifles, some as exercises, others voluntarily—for poetry was now become my delight—and not a few at the desire of my friends. When I became capable, however, of reading Latin and Greek with some degree of facility, that gentleman employed all my leisure hours in translations from the classics. Among others "Juvenal" engaged my attention, and I translated the tenth satire for a holiday task. Mr. Smerdon was much pleased with this, and easily persuaded me to proceed, and I translated four more satires. On my removing to Exeter College, my friend advised me to present my translation of the tenth satire to the Rev. Dr. Stinton, to whom Mr. Taylor had given me an introductory letter. I did so, and it was kindly received. Thus encouraged, I took up the first and second satires, when my friend, who had sedulously watched my progress, started the idea of going through the whole and publishing it by subscription, for increasing my means of subsistence."

This undertaking was accordingly set on foot, and a subscription list was opened. Mr. Cookesley, who was a man of taste and judgment, undertook the task of revising the whole translation; but before the completion of the first satire, this truly excellent man died very suddenly, leaving his young *protégé* overwhelmed with grief; nor was his sorrow a transient emotion:—

"Twenty years," he writes, "have elapsed since I lost my benefactor and my friend. In the interval I have wept a thousand times at the recollection of his goodness: I yet cherish his memory with filial respect, and at this distant period my heart sinks within me at every repetition of his name."

In vain did Gifford attempt to resume the translation of "Juvenal." Every effort proved abortive, and brought with it such bitter anguish, from the sense of his loss, that he was compelled to abandon the work, which was not completed till after he had long attained to competence and scholastic fame.

At this crisis a fortunate accident introduced him, not long after the decease of his first patron, to Lord Grosvenor, who proved a more efficient, though not a more sincere friend. On his first visit to this nobleman :—

"He asked me what friends I had, and what were my prospects in life; and I told him that I had no friends and no prospects of any kind. He said no more; but when I called to take leave, previous to returning to college, I found that this simple exposure of my circumstances had sunk deep into his mind. At parting he informed me that he charged himself with my present support and future establishment; and that till this last could be effected to my wish, I should come and reside with him. These were not words of course: they were more than fulfilled in every point. I did go and reside with him, and I experienced a warm and cordial reception, a kind and affectionate esteem that has known neither diminution nor interruption from that hour to this, a period of twenty years!

"In his lordship's house I proceeded with 'Juvenal,' till I was called upon to accompany his son to the Continent. With him, in two successive tours, I spent many years; years of which the remembrance will always be dear to me, from the recollection that a friendship was then contracted which time and a more intimate knowledge of each other have mellowed into a regard that forms at once the pride and happiness of my life."

In this manner closes Mr. Gifford's autobiographical narrative, first published with his "Juvenal," in 1802. He had then already acquired great celebrity as the author of the "Baviad" and the "Mœviad," though he makes no allusion to either of these works in his narrative.

These satires were directed against the follies and extravagance of what was then called the Della Cruscan style of poetry, and the vitiated state of the modern drama. The peculiar talent displayed in these productions showed that their author had imbibed somewhat of the spirit of his early favourite, "Juvenal," and the stinging sarcasm of the Latin poet was doubtless keenly appreciated by one who proved himself so mighty to wield the powerful and ready pen of the satirist and critic.

His known ability soon recommended him to the notice of Mr. Canning, who, in 1797, started a paper styled the *Anti-Jacobin*, of which Gifford, who entered with his whole heart into the views of the Anti-Gallican party, was appointed the editor. This connection introduced him to the most brilliant circles of political and literary men, with many of whom he formed friendships, especially with Mr. Pitt, of whom he was a devoted admirer, and in later years an intimate friend. In 1809 the *Quarterly Review* was established, and he was selected to conduct that celebrated journal, of which he continued the editor till within a year of his death. Under his auspices its success was most brilliant, and undoubtedly he was admirably fitted for this employment. He felt strongly and wrote powerfully. There were gall and wormwood in his pen—but no bitterness in his spirit—said all who knew the man.

One who wrote of him after years of observation and friendship, pronounced him "good, mild, and overflowing with gentle affections." If the literary and political judge were severe, the man, in private life, was benevolent and tender-hearted.

That he had the power of feeling and inspiring strong friendships the history of his life proves. His gratitude to Mr. Cookesley was ardent, and ended only with his existence; indeed, he left the bulk of his fortune to that gentleman's son.

For his pupil, Lord Grosvenor, he formed an attachment which no subsequent circumstances could abate; and how sincerely this affection was reciprocated, we learn from an incident related by his biographer. In Mr. Gifford's last painful and protracted illness, when he was asleep during the greater part of the day, Lord Grosvenor occasionally ventured to infringe his strict orders not to be disturbed, and walking on tiptoe to his side, would stand and gaze on his almost expiring instructor.

Mr. Gifford died in London on the 31st December 1826, in the seventy-first year of his age, and was buried in Westminster Abbey, immediately below the monuments of Camden and Garrick. The following lines were written by his friend John Taylor, Esq. :—

> " At rest is Gifford! from a lowly state
> He rose, to rank among the truly great.
> His youth in penury and pain was past,
> And Fate's dark clouds seemed menacing to last;
> But though he drooped beneath a load of care,
> He sunk not in the depths of dire despair:
> Still 'mid coarse drudgery and tyrant sway
> His mind was cheered by learning's dawning ray.
>
> * * * *
>
> Mild was his temper; if severe his pen
> 'Twas only aimed at vain and vicious men;
> Firm to support those principles alone
> That shield the people and uphold the throne,
> In him the critic, scholar, bard combined
> With zeal intrepid and a candid mind."

James Ferguson.

WHEN admiring the works of some skilful mechanic or artisan, the wish must often arise in one's mind—Would that the man had given us the story of his life, of the manner in which he first began and afterwards prosecuted his studies, till he attained to such admirable perfection in his art. Occasionally this wish is gratified, and we have a genuine autobiography of a man of native ability, who has overcome all the obstacles of poverty and neglected education by the efforts of his genius and industry.

Such a narrative we have from the pen of James Ferguson, a man to whom the mechanics of this country owe a large debt of gratitude, since to his labours may be in part attributed the now general distribution of scientific knowledge among them. "It seems," says Sir D. Brewster, "to have been the chief object of Ferguson's writings to give a familiar view of the various branches of physical science, and to render them accessible to those not accustomed to mathematical investigation; and the favourable reception which his works have everywhere experienced is a satisfactory proof that he did not labour in vain." Of his "Lectures on Mechanics," the same authority says, "No book whatever upon the same subject has been so generally read, and so widely circulated among all classes. We meet with it in the workshop of every mechanic. We find it transfused into many of the Encyclopædias which this country has produced, and we may easily trace it in those popular systems of philosophy which have lately appeared." The early history of this remarkable man he himself relates as follows:—"I was born in the year 1710, a few miles from Keith, a little village in Banffshire, in the north of Scotland, and can with pleasure say that my parents, though poor, were religious and honest, lived in good repute with all who knew them, and died with good characters.

"As my father had nothing to support a large family but his daily labour, it was not to be expected that he could bestow much on the education of his children, yet they were not neglected, for, at his leisure hours, he taught them to read and write. It was while he was teaching my elder brother to read the Scotch Catechism that I acquired my reading. Ashamed to ask my father to instruct me, I used, when he and my brother were abroad, to take the Catechism and study the lesson which he had been teaching my brother, and when any difficulty occurred, I went to a neighbouring old woman, who gave me such help as enabled me to read tolerably well before my father had thought of teaching me. Some time after he was agreeably surprised to find me reading by myself; he thereupon gave me further instruction, and also taught me to write, which, with about three months I afterwards had at the grammar school at Keith, was all the education I ever received.

"My taste for mechanics arose from an odd accident. When I was about seven or eight years of age, a part of the roof of the house being decayed, my father, desirous of mending it, applied a prop and lever to an upright spar to raise it to its former situation, and to my great astonishment I saw him lift up the ponderous roof as if it had been a small weight. I attributed this at first to a degree of strength that excited my terror as well as wonder; but thinking further of the matter, I recollected that he had applied his strength to that part of the lever which was furthest from the prop, and finding on inquiry that this was the means by which the seeming wonder was effected, I began making levers, and by applying weights to them in different ways, I found the power gained by my lever was just in proportion to the lengths of the different parts of the lever on either side of the prop. I then thought it was a great pity that by this means a weight could be raised only a very little way. On this I soon imagined that, by pulling round a wheel, the weight might be raised to any height by tying a rope to the weight and winding the rope round the axle of the wheel, and that the power gained must be just as great as the wheel was broader than the axle was thick, and found it to be exactly so by hanging one weight to a rope put round the wheel and another to the rope that coiled round the axle. . . . . . . By means of a turning-lathe which my father had and sometimes used, and a little knife, I was enabled to make the wheels and other things necessary for my purpose.

"I then wrote a short account of these machines, and sketched out figures of them with a pen, imagining it to be the first treatise of the kind that ever was written. From that time my mind preserved a constant tendency to improve in that science. But as my father could not afford to maintain me while I was in pursuit only of these matters, he put me to a neighbour to keep sheep, which I continued to do for some years; and in that time I began to study the stars in the night. In the day time I amused myself by making models of mills, spinning-wheels, and such other things as I happened to see. I then went to serve a considerable farmer in the neighbourhood, whose name was James Glashan. I found him very kind and indulgent, but he soon observed that, in the evenings, when my work was over, I went into a field with a blanket about me, lay down on my back, and stretched a thread with small beads upon it till they hid such and such stars from my

FERGUSON TAKING THE DISTANCE OF THE STARS.

eye in order to take their apparent distances from one another, and then, laying the thread down on a paper, I marked the stars thereon by the beads according to their respective positions, having a candle by me. My master at first laughed at me, but when I explained my meaning to him, he encouraged me to go on; and that I might make fair copies in the daytime of what I had done in the night, he often worked for me himself. *I shall always have a respect for the memory of that man.*

"One day he sent me with a message to Mr. J. Gilchrist, minister at Keith, to whom I had been known from my childhood. I carried my star papers to show him, and found him looking over a large parcel of maps, which I surveyed with great pleasure as they were the first I had ever seen. He then told me the earth is round like a ball, and explained the map of it to me. I requested him to lend me *that* map to take a copy of it in the evenings, for which pleasant employment my master gave me more time than I could reasonably expect, and often took the threshing-flail out of my hands and worked himself, while I sat by him in the barn busy with my compasses, ruler, and pen. When I had finished the copy I asked leave to carry home the map. In my way to the minister's house I happened to pass by the village school, where I saw a genteel-looking man painting a sun-dial on the wall. I stopped awhile to observe him, and the schoolmaster came out and asked me what parcel it was I had under my arm. I showed him the map and my copy of it, wherewith he appeared very well pleased, and asked me whether I should not like to learn of Mr. Cantley to make sun-dials. Mr. Cantley then looked at the copy of the map, and commended it much. I had a good deal of conversation with him, and found him affable and communicative, which made me wish I could be further acquainted with him.

"I then proceeded with the map to the minister, and while we were conversing together a neighbouring gentleman, Thomas Grant, Esq. of Achoynaney, happened to come in. The minister introduced me, and showed him what I had done; he expressed great satisfaction, asked me some questions, and told me that if I would go and live at his house he would order his butler, Alexander Cantley, to give me a great deal of instruction. Finding this was the man whom I had seen painting the sun-dial, I told Squire Grant that I should rejoice to be at his house as soon as the time was expired for which I was engaged to my present master.

"When the term of my servitude was out I left my good master and went to the gentleman's house, where I quickly found myself with a most humane good family. Mr. Cantley, the butler, soon became my friend, and continued so till his death. He was the most extraordinary man that I ever was acquainted with, or perhaps ever shall see; for he was a complete master of arithmetic, a good mathematician, a master of music on every known instrument except the harp, understood Latin, French, and Greek, and could prescribe as a physician upon an urgent occasion. He was what is generally called *self-taught*, but I think he might with much greater propriety have been termed God Almighty's scholar. He taught me much, but to my inexpressible grief, just as he was beginning to instruct me in the elements of geometry, he left Mr. Grant, and went to live at several miles distance. The good family could not prevail with me to stay after he left, so I quitted them and went to my father's, but as he had, without my assistance, hands sufficient for all his work, I went to a miller, thinking it would be a very easy business to attend the mill, and that I should have a great deal of leisure for my studies."

He soon discovered his mistake; the man in whose service he had engaged himself proved utterly worthless and unfeeling, and at the end of a year Ferguson left him much injured in health by starvation and over-work. His next situation was even worse. At the end of three months he again returned home disabled and penniless, and for several months he continued too unwell to think of engaging himself again.

"In order to amuse myself in this low state," he continues, "I made a wooden clock, the frame of which was also of wood, and it kept time pretty well. The bell on which the hammer struck the hours was the neck of a broken bottle. Having then no idea how any time-keeper could go but by a weight and a line, I wondered how a watch could go in all positions; but happening one day to see a gentleman ride by my father's house, I asked him what o'clock it then was. He looked at his watch and told me, and he did that with so much good nature, that I begged him to show me the inside of his watch, and though he was an entire stranger he instantly opened the watch and put it into my hands."

In reply to the lad's eager inquiries, this benevolent stranger then explained to him the construction of the works, and patiently continued his instructions till Ferguson, thanking him, told him that he understood the thing very well. "I then," continues his narrative, "tried to make a watch with wooden wheels, and made the spring of whalebone. I enclosed the whole in a wooden case very little bigger than a breakfast tea-cup, but a clumsy neighbour one day looking at my watch, happened to let it fall, and turning hastily to pick it up, set his foot upon it and crushed it all to pieces, which so provoked my father that he was almost ready to beat the man, and discouraged me so much that I never attempted to make such another machine.

"As soon as I was able to go abroad, I carried my globe and other things to Sir James Dunbar of Durn, as I had heard he was a very good-natured, friendly, inquisitive gentleman. He received me in a very kind manner, was pleased with what I showed him, and desired I would clean his clocks. This, for the first time, I attempted, and then began to pick up some money in that way about the country, making Sir James's house my home at his desire."

Here the ingenious lad soon found new exercise for his wits:—"Two large globular stones stood on

PAINTING THE GLOBES. 293

FERGUSON PAINTING THE GLOBES.

the top of his gate, on one of them I painted with oil colours, a map of the terrestrial globe, and on the other a map of the celestial. The poles of the painted globes stood toward the poles of the heavens; on each the twenty-four hours were placed around the equinoctial, so as to show the time of day when the sun shone out by the boundary where the half of the globe, at any time enlightened by the sun, was parted from the other half in the shade, the enlightened parts of the terrestrial globe answering to the like enlightened parts of the earth at all times. So that, whenever the sun shone on the globe, one might see to what places the sun was then rising, to what places it was setting, and all the places where it was then day or night throughout the earth."

While Ferguson was staying at Sir James Dunbar's, that kind and generous patron introduced him to his sister, Lady Dipple. This lady asked him if he thought he could make patterns for needlework on aprons and gowns, and having been shown some, he soon succeeded in producing others after his own fancy, which found favour with the ladies of the neighbourhood, and sold for so much money as seemed to him quite a little fortune. "By this means I had," he says, "the pleasure of occasionally supplying the wants of my poor father. All this while, however, I could not leave off star-gazing in the nights, and taking the places of the planets among the stars, by my thread. Thus I could observe how the planets changed their places among the stars, and I delineated their paths on the celestial map, which I had copied from the above mentioned celestial globe."

In Sir James's house were many pictures and prints, which he set himself to copy in pen and ink, and being introduced by Lady Dipple to her son-in-law, William Baird, Esq., that gentleman was so much pleased with his efforts, that he took him to his residence, and gave him much useful instruction and assistance. By his advice Ferguson began to take likenesses, and his success in this new occupation appeared so satisfactory to Mr. Baird and Lady Dipple that they determined he should go to Edinburgh and be regularly instructed in the art of portrait painting. When he reached the Scotch capital he was, however, much disconcerted on finding that no painter would consent to receive him as an apprentice without a premium.

"Being," as he says, " quite at a loss what to do," he went with a letter of recommendation from his friend Squire Baird to the Rev. Dr. Keith, who, on hearing his tale, bade him take courage and rely on his own practice; and that if he would copy from nature he might succeed very well. He then sat to the young artist for his own picture, and recommended him to the notice of the two Ladies Douglas, who lived near Edinburgh, and by whose friendly assistance he soon procured as much business in the portrait painting way as he could possibly execute, put a good deal of money into his pocket, and was able to spare sufficient for the supply of his excellent parents in their old age.

"Thus," he continues, "was a business providentially put into my hands, which I followed for twenty-six years.

"In the meantime, Lady Dipple, being a woman of the strictest piety, kept a watchful eye over me at first, and made me give her an exact account at night of what families I had been in throughout the day, and of the money I had received. She took the money each night, desiring I would keep an account of what I had put into her hands, telling me I should duly have out of it, what I wanted for clothes, and to send to my father. But, in less than half a year, she told me she would thenceforth trust me to be my own banker, for she had made private inquiry how I had behaved when out of her sight, and was satisfied with my conduct."

Portrait-painting, however, was not Ferguson's true vocation, and he felt it. He became anxious to try some other branch of art, and for awhile studied medicine, but soon relinquished it, and returned to his first and true bent—the study of astronomy, regretting heartily that he had neglected it so long.

At the age of twenty-nine he married; and the year following, with very scanty data, and hardly any supply of books and instruments, to assist him, he invented an excellent machine for showing the new moons and eclipses, which he called the Astronomical Rotula. This, when completed, he sent to the celebrated Maclaurin, who on examination found it very nearly correct, and was so well pleased with the ingenuity it evinced that from that time he became the friend of Ferguson, and continued so till his death.

Here was a patron well qualified to assist him in his philosophical studies and kindly disposed to do so. "One day," says our author, "I requested him to show me his orrery which he immediately did. I was greatly delighted with the motions of the earth and moon in it; and would gladly have seen the wheel box, which was concealed in a brass box. But he told me he had never opened it; and I could easily perceive it could not be done without a great deal of time and trouble.

"After a good deal of thinking and calculation, I found that I could contrive the planets in such a machine and giving them their progressive motions; I then employed a turner to make me a sufficient number of wheels and axles according to patterns which I gave him in drawing, and having put the whole together I found it answered all my expectations. When it was completed I showed it to Mr. Maclaurin who commended it to the young gentlemen who attended his lectures, and desired me to read them a lecture on it, which I did without any hesitation, seeing I had no reason to be afraid of speaking before a great and good man who was my friend.

"I then made a smaller and neater orrery, of which all the wheels were of ivory, and I have made six orreries since, but there are not any two of them in which the wheelwork is alike, for I could never bear to copy one thing of that kind from another, because I still saw there was great room for improvements."

By a letter of recommendation from Mr. Baron Edlin of Edinburgh, Ferguson was made acquainted with the Honourable Stephen Pointz, Esq., who showed him much kindness, and whom he mentions with the utmost gratitude and veneration.

Shortly after, he came under the notice of the Royal Society in the following manner:—"It appeared to me, on consideration that, although the moon goes round the earth and that the sun is far on the outside of the moon's orbit, yet the moon's motion must be in a line that is always concave toward the sun; and on examination, I found it to be really so. I then made a simple machine for delineating both her path and the earth's on a long paper laid on the floor. I carried the machine and delineation to the late Martin Folkes, Esq., President of the Royal Society; and he expressed great satisfaction at seeing it, as it was a new discovery. He took me with him that evening to the Royal Society where I showed the delineation and the method of doing it."

In the year 1747 he published his first work, a "Dissertation on the Phenomena of the Harvest Moon" with the description of a new orrery, having only four wheels. With characteristic modesty, he says,—"Having never had grammatical education nor time to study the rules of just composition, I acknowledge that I was afraid to put it to the press; and for the same cause I ought to have the same fears still. But, having the pleasure to find that this, my first work, was not ill received, I was emboldened to go on, in publishing my astronomy, mechanical lectures, tables and tracts relative to several arts and sciences, the young gentleman's and lady's astronomy, a small treatise on electricity, and the following sheets" (his select mechanical exercises).

The narrative—which here closes—has been given entire, with the exception of a few passages; since, how could it be possible to give so correct and pleasant an impression of the mind of the man, as do these simple pages? From the time of his establishment in London, Ferguson's career was a successful one. When he published the preceding autobiography he had lived thirty years in the metropolis, and he tells us, that, during all that time he had met with the strongest marks of friendship from all ranks of people in town and country. In the year 1763, he was elected a member of the Royal Society without paying for admission, an honour very rarely conferred on Englishmen, and strongly marking the estimation in which he was held by that learned body. Several of his works were translated into the French, German, and Swedish languages; and thus his fame as a popular writer was extended beyond his native country. George III., took great pleasure in conversing with Ferguson on scientific subjects, distinguished him by numerous marks of favour, and gave him, from his privy purse, a pension of £50 per annum.

After a long and useful life, unhappy in his domestic connections, in a feeble and precarious state of health, worn out with study, age, and infirmities, he died on the 16th November, 1776; he was no more than sixty-six years of age, but he looked considerably older.

Ferguson was a man of very clear judgment, and of unwearied application to study; benevolent, meek, and innocent in his manners as a child; humble, courteous, and communicative. His religious character gave the tone to his general conduct. The anxieties and changes of his chequered life never effaced the religious impressions early produced by the piety of his parents, but rather strengthened his confidence towards God, and his belief in the great doctrines of our most holy faith.

A lovely character was his, according to the testimony of all who knew him.

Sir Robert Strange.

WHAT lover of the delightful art of engraving but feels ready to doff his cap at mention of the name of Strange, the father of the art in England as he has been deservedly styled, a man, too, whose history has a touch of the romantic about it. The early part of his life was full of adventure, for the skilful hand which rendered with ingenious skill the master-pieces of Guido and Titian, also engraved the plates of Jacobite bank notes and waved a broad sword in the fight of Culloden.

He was born in the island of Pomona in the Orkneys, and has given a lively, though unhappily an incomplete memoir of himself. His father, he tells us, was descended from an ancient family in the county of Fife; his mother the daughter of a gentleman named Scollay living in the Orkneys. In his earlier years he received such education as the country afforded, and which terminated in an excellent grammar-school, where he attained some general knowledge of the classics. His father dying when he was young, it became necessary that he should betake himself to some regular course of life. His natural inclination was for the sea; for, having been accustomed to take his pleasure on the water and to visit many of the vessels which arrived or took their departure, he had experienced the sweets but none of the hardships of the watery element.

The account, given by himself of his boyish proceedings is lively and natural:—"I had frequently been accustomed to amuse myself with drawing, without knowing its tendency, for never had an idea of art passed the Pentland Firth. Living in a remote corner of the world, genius had not here its proper latitude either for exertion or information.

"My relations in general combated every idea I entertained with respect to the sea; the law was what they had held out to me, which, after some difficulty, and having no other alternative, I of course agreed to. Soon after this, I was placed with an intelligent man, an attorney. I had not been long there before my time began to hang heavy on my hands; the task assigned me was in copying papers which I but little understood; of course they could afford me no entertainment. In this manner did I rub over several months, neither to my own, nor to the satisfaction of others."

Happily for him the youth had a half-brother who, for several years, had been settled at Edinburgh, as a writer or lawyer. It was determined that this relative should be consulted as to his future course, and the result was that in a short time he was despatched to Auld Reekie, where his kind-hearted brother received him with the utmost affection. "Tears of gratitude at this moment bedew my cheeks, and whilst breathing I must venerate his memory—(says the warm-hearted man, when recalling to mind his youthful days). He proved indeed, in the sequel, a true father to me; and finding that I had the same propensity as ever for going to sea, he one morning put the question to me, 'Robie, how would you like to go on board a man-of-war?" I replied there was nothing I should like better. He then told me that he had mentioned me to Captain Robinson, the commander of the *Alborough* man-of-war, a vessel of twenty guns, at this time stationed in the road of Leith, who informed him that he was going upon a cruise for some weeks, during which he had no objection to receive me on board his ship, and that after his return I might either remain or leave the vessel if I found the sea was not agreeable to me. No proposal could be more flattering than this; I was elated with it beyond measure."

This trial trip produced an entire change in the feelings of young Strange; the weather he encountered was very severe, and though he had the honour of forming part of the convoy of the Swedish Ambassador on his return to Gottenburg, he was only too happy to find himself restored to *terra firma*.

"Before leaving Gottenburg," he continues, "I had

wrote a letter to my brother, in which I was not altogether that enthusiast I had been in favour of my new profession; for this time I had begun to state, as debtor and creditor, both the pleasures and hardships which attended this course of life. My friend, Mr. Sommers (one of the midshipmen) contributed not a little to unhinge me by stating to me his own grievances and the precariousness of promotion in the service. His words frequently were, 'Bob, if you have any other alternative, quit the sea, and you'll afterwards bless me for my advice.' Time did indeed verify it.

"Our passage back to England seemed to me as tedious as it had been to Sweden. It was now late in the season, and we had reason to apprehend the equinoctial storms, which, indeed, we soon experienced. They were both violent and of long duration. For many days our fire was extinguished, the guns lashed, the topmasts lowered, the sails furled, and the vessel herself left to the fury of a merciless element. All this while I was sick to death, and ever wishing myself on shore. . . The day after our arrival I landed, blessing my stars on so happy an event, and congratulating myself for the first fortunate period of my life which restored me to an affectionate brother, and from whom I received the kindest welcome."

It will be readily believed that, from this time no thought of a seafaring life ever crossed the mind of the youth. He now listened with willing and grateful ears to the proposal that he should follow the profession of the law under his brother's auspices. "Before leaving my native country," he says, "I had wrote an excellent hand of write, but had been out of the practice of it for several months. It was not to be doubted that I should soon recover it, and which was actually the case, for I soon became extremely useful. My brother attended at this time a public office where he spent the morning till towards the hour of dinner. I generally occupied his apartment at home, where I employed my time in copying such papers as he had occasion for. In this manner the winter passed over, though not without some little encroachments on my part upon the time I should have employed in my avocation. These were briefly no other than that I had begun, as it were in a private way, to amuse myself with drawing; keeping everything, however, as much as I could out of sight.

One day it chanced my brother came in, rather by times, and sent me some messages which occupied a considerable part of the afternoon. During my absence he rummaged for some papers in the bureau at which I used to write, where unfortunately he put his hand upon a budget of drawings I had carefully concealed. They were no more than little sketches I had done in pen and ink: some few from my own fancy; and others from the ornaments and title pages of books, &c. On my return I little dreamt of this detection, nor did I even suspect it. No conduct on the part of my brother afforded me the least hint. He had removed the drawings, and afterwards converted them to my advantage."

Cooper, the engraver, was then residing at Edinburgh, and to him the little hoarded treasure was shown: he thought the sketches promised well; and offered, through his brother, to Strange's great delight, to make trial of the lad, in case he were desirous to become an engraver. The legal copying was speedily thrown aside, and in due course Strange was apprenticed to his new master for a period of six years. The autobiography continues:—" I was now totally removed to Mr. Cooper's, where I insensibly became one of the family, and a favourite too. I felt my situation easy, and the love of my profession grew upon me, more or less, every day. Nature had here her full scope, and genius soon began to exert itself. The line which Mr. Cooper pursued was engraving, this art having been almost totally unknown. Of one kind and another he had a multiplicity of work, though not of the first choice. He had employed an artist or two he had brought down from London, and besides myself, he had other apprentices. A school of this kind could not fail of communicating, as it were, the first rudiments of the art, where the assiduity of the young artist was perpetually employed and solicitous of doing well. My master encouraged me as much as possible in the study of drawing, he was exceedingly communicative, and on all occasions opened to me his portfolios. In short, I soon became of real utility to him, and was, of course, a favourite. Among other advantages, we had a winter's academy at Edinburgh, on which I became a constant attendant. I had likewise copied some French prints, which gave me a facility with the graver, intermixing that harmony which the exercise of drawing will ever produce in the execution of any subject, but particularly that of history, to which I had ever an eye.

"In this manner passed the two first years of my apprenticeship, when an event happened, which proved to me one of the greatest misfortunes I have experienced in life; it was the death of my brother, who was cut off in the flower of life, and in the course of a few days, by a violent fever. I not only lost on this occasion a brother, but a second father, a friend and a benefactor. There were united in him all the qualities of the best of hearts. He was generous, he was benevolent, and he was humane."

There is something very beautiful in this touching tribute to fraternal affection. So cordial an attachment on the part of the elder brother for his young and inexperienced charge, combined with so much prudence and sagacity in his management of the lad, deserved the reward they earned in his lively and enduring gratitude. What a model for the imitation of brothers, who may be in similar circumstances, and how instructive, in many ways, are these simple records of family affection which chance occasionally gives to light. Dear and blessed are the charities of blood and home, and God means they should be so. "Let brotherly love continue," should ever be the motto of the domestic hearth.

This unexpected calamity for a time unsettled the mind of Strange. He felt a lingering after his early home, and begged for leave of absence. To this his master was averse, but the desire became more strong, until it resembled what the French call "la maladie du pays." Mr. Cooper was compelled to yield to the urgency of his pupil, who lost no time in sailing for the Orkneys, where the tears and embraces of his mother comforted his sorrowful heart, and after a season restored him to cheerfulness. It was natural and fitting that, being now thrown entirely on his own resources, he should look about him and consider how he might best carve his fortune and earn the means of independence.

"I had now," he says, "been upwards of three years absent from my native country; my reputation as an artist had found its way even to the Orkneys,—an appellation which for the first time had been heard of in the country. Many in consequence were desirous of possessing something of my engraving, whether in seals, crests, coats of arms, &c. During my stay, and in visiting several gentlemen in the islands, I was charged with a number of commissions, which my employers in general were anxious to possess; this occasioned a prolongation of my absence from Edinburgh. On my return I resumed with all the ardour in my power my former avocations. Mr. Cooper had engaged in a new work which was the folio edition of Albinus's Anatomical Plates; I had in some measure the conducting of the work, and even my choice of such subjects as I wished to engrave; what fell to my province was the osteology, and two plates of the external muscles. This work did not fail to be a considerable advantage to me. . . . . I now applied to Mr. Cooper, that he would indulge me occasionally with a day or two to execute a few of the commissions I had brought with me from the Orkneys, and others I had received elsewhere, telling him that he could not be a stranger to the fact that my brother's death had been the greatest misfortune to me, and that I could not subsist, nor make a decent appearance in the world without some resource of the nature I was now proposing; that I had already borrowed some money of my mother, which she could but ill spare, having still a numerous family to support; and that I had given her a security upon the property which she now life-rented, to be paid her upon my coming of age. I added that I should keep a regular account of the time I might have occasion to encroach upon, and that I should faithfully make it up to him at the expiration of my indentures. All this was in the natural order of things, and actually happened." Strange's apprenticeship ended in 1741. The rapid progress he had made under the instructions of his master, fully satisfied his friends that, in making choice of a profession, he had followed the bent of nature, and was pursuing the career for which his genius fitted him. But while he was thus assiduously employed in laying the foundation of his future fame, unforeseen occurrences gave a new turn to his history, and eventually opened to him a wider and more promising career in the cultivation of his art. These circumstances arose out of the Jacobite rebellion of 1745, which for the time made Strange a soldier, although, according to his biographer, "his entanglement in the Stuart cause arose neither from youthful enthusiasm, hereditary prepossessions, nor earnest conviction." He was, in reality, influenced by the smiles of a fair lady, to whom he had become attached, and whose ardour in the cause of the young Chevalier, was so intense that she made it a condition with her lover, (betrothed to her at the time), that he should fight for the Prince. Once engaged in the cause, he bore himself gallantly. He joined the rebel army, and continued to act with it, as one of the corps styled the Life Guards,—a post of danger as well as of honour,—and in this capacity was present at Culloden. Previous to this, while the Prince was at Edinburgh, he engraved a half-length portrait of him looking out of an oval,

STRANGE ARMING FOR THE WARS.

with the motto, *everso missus succurrere seclo*. This, which is Strange's earliest known work on his own account, was regarded as a wonder of art by the followers of the Chevalier, and probably procured him the commission to engrave a plate for their bank notes. On the evening of a ball at Inverness, he was sent for to the Prince's bedchamber, to exhibit his device for that purpose. On this occasion he says,—

"I then proceeded towards explaining what I had in view, and with that intention, pulled out of my pocket a small device I had put together; the better to communicate my ideas. It consisted, I said, of nothing but the slightest compartment, from behind which a rose issued on one side, and a thistle on the other, as mere ornamental; the interior part I meant should be filled up by clerks with the specific sums which were intended, &c.; and I proposed etching or engraving, in the slightest manner for expedition, a considerable repetition of this ornament on two plates, for the facility of printing, that such should be done on the strongest paper, so that when cut separate, they should resist, in some measure, the wear they must sustain in the common use of circulation. The Prince had at this time taken it out of my hand, and was showing it to Mr. Murray, and seemed much pleased with the idea of the rose and thistle. In short, everything was approved of, and the utmost expedition recommended me.

"We now talked of a circulation of larger sums, which would likewise be required. I gave it as my opinion that they could not do better than issue notes in imitation of the Bank of England, or the Royal Bank of Scotland, in the execution of which

THE ENGRAVER AND THE PRINCE.

there was very little labour; that it would be necessary, if possible, to see such notes, in order to concert a form how they were to be drawn up, by whom paid, or at what period; if at a given time, that of the

Restoration I imagined would be the properest. This produced a general smile."

He afterwards procured a coppersmith, and with his help was ready in a fortnight to begin printing. On his next visit to Culloden House, his companions jokingly asked him when they were to have any of his money. "I replied, that if they gave a good account of the Duke (meaning Cumberland), I hoped his treasury-chest would supply us."

Two or three days later the battle of Culloden was fought. Strange was present, and took part in the affair, of which he has given a very spirited account; the result was precisely what might have been anticipated from the wretched state of the troops, who, for many weeks before the fight, had been reduced to a short allowance of bread (or rather oatmeal, for they had no other), and were worn out with fatigue, destitute of the common necessaries of life, and outnumbered upwards of two to one by their enemies. The contest was not of long duration, and the discomfited cavaliers speedily quitted the field. Strange thus paints the scene:—

"The confusion was now great, nor can the imagination figure it. The men in general were betaking themselves precipitately to flight, nor was there any possibility of their being rallied. Horror and dismay were painted in every countenance. It now became time to provide for the Prince's safety; his person had been abundantly exposed. He was got off the field, and very narrowly escaped falling in with a body of horse, which had been detached from the Duke's left, were advancing with an incredible rapidity, picking up the stragglers, and as they gave no quarter, were levelling them with the ground. The greater number of the army were already out of danger, the flight having been so precipitate. We got upon a rising ground, where we turned round and made a general halt. The scene was, indeed, tremendous. Never was so total a rout—a more thorough discomfiture of an army. The adjacent country was in a manner covered with its ruins. The whole was over in about twenty-five minutes. The Duke's artillery kept still playing, though not a soul upon the field. His army was kept together, all but the horse. The great pursuit was upon the road towards Inverness. Of towards six thousand men, which the Prince's army at this time consisted of, about one thousand were asleep in Culloden parks, who knew nothing of the action till awakened by the noise of the cannon. These in general tried to save themselves by taking the road towards Inverness, and most of them fell a sacrifice to the victors, for the road was in general strewed with dead bodies. The Prince at this moment had his cheek bedewed with tears; what must not his feeling heart have suffered!"

After the catastrophe, Strange, like many of his fellow soldiers, was obliged to fly for shelter to the mountains, where he continued for several months, enduring various hardships. Little is known of the incidents which befell him during this eventful period of his career. One anecdote has been preserved, given on the authority of his quondam instructor Cooper. On one occasion, when hotly pressed, he dashed into a room, where the lady whose zeal had enlisted him in the fatal cause, sat singing at her needlework. Failing other means of concealment, her prompt intervention came to his assistance; she wore, as was the fashion of the day, a large hoop, which she quickly raised, and the affianced lover disappeared beneath its ample shelter, and thanks to the self-possession of the dame, who continued with unfaltering notes to chant her ditty, he lay undetected, while the rude and baffled soldiery vainly ransacked the house.

How narrowly Strange escaped the fatalities of war, we learn from the following accident. Having been employed to execute some military order in the absence of an aide-de-camp, he was riding for the purpose along the shore, when the sword which he carried was bent in his hand by a ball from one of the king's vessels stationed off the coast. The vigilance of pursuit being somewhat abated, he left the Highlands and returned to Edinburgh, where, for the first time, he began to turn his talents to account, contriving to maintain himself in concealment by the sale of small drawings of the rival leaders in the rebellion, which were purchased at the time in great numbers, at a guinea each. A fan also, which he had intended for his fair preserver, and on which he had accordingly bestowed more than usual pains, was sold at this time, with a sad heart, to supply his pressing necessities.

Tired of a life of alarm and privacy, he at length procured a safe-conduct to London, intending, as soon as practicable, to embark for France; but not before he had secured the prize for the sake of which he had risked his life in the field.

The name of the lady to whom he was united, was Isabella Lumisden. She was the daughter of an old and respectable family, and in her steady affection through a long and chequered life, her husband was amply rewarded for the perils he encountered as her lover. No particulars of their marriage are preserved, but family tradition says that, the father of the lady being obdurately opposed to a match of so quixotic a nature—(for how were the young couple to live?) the pair assumed the guidance of their own destiny, and crowned it by a "clandestine union." The affair took place early in 1747; it seems to have been a highly imprudent and rash step, and Strange's long absences on his professional duties sadly marred through life the domestic comforts which they might have enjoyed, had not their straitened circumstances interfered.

From this time the particulars of our artist's life are principally obtained from the letters of his wife and her brother Mr. Andrew Lumisden. This gentleman was an equally strong Jacobite with his sister, and was so deeply compromised in the rebellion, that he was excepted by name from the Act of Grace. He escaped in the disguise of a groom, "his yellow locks having been replaced by a black wig, with eyebrows corked to the proper tinge." Afterwards he assumed the garb of a poor teacher in rusty black garments and bushy periwig, carrying in his pocket a tiny Virgil and Horace. Finally, he embarked at the Tower Stairs, and got safe to Rouen. His circumstances were so indifferent that he soon wrote home saying he was "in a starving condition." His father being slow to supply his necessities, he vainly endeavoured to get into trade, but ultimately became secretary to the Chevalier at Rome, in whose service he continued for sixteen years—in short, till the death of his master. In his latter days he obtained a pardon and returned to Edinburgh. His letters, together with Mrs. Strange's, extending over the greater part of his life, show a strong affection for Strange, or "Robie," as they both called him. At his suggestion eighteen months after his marriage, Strange went to Rouen, to study drawing under Descamps, professor of design in that city; and his wife, writing to her brother on the occasion says, "Before receiving your last, Robie was resolved to have gone directly to Rome, to have studied miniature painting, but he is now determined to spend most of his time with you, as drawing is what he chiefly wants. The nearer he is, I'll be the better pleased. The best of it will be hard enough on me, for I am convinced there never was a happier pair. With great pleasure would I go along with him, but am afraid I would be too heavy a cloak bag; so must even content myself with my bonny little Mary, till my dear Robie returns." The happiness of the young wife had recently been completed by the birth of a daughter, to whom she thus prettily refers.

From Rouen Strange went to Paris, where he worked with Le Bas. He gained the first prize at the Academy of Design in that city, and thereupon resolved to make engraving his principal business, and miniature painting his second.

Lumisden from time to time reported what progress he was making, and praised the goodness and sweetness of his temper, which he described as conciliating everybody. His affectionate wife in return commends her "dearest" to the care of her brother, as "entitled to the esteem of every true Briton," and charges him to see that he takes reasonable recreation —fencing, dancing, running, or riding, and "now and then a glass of wine will do him no harm."

Brave hearted little woman! At this very time —as she related in more prosperous days—she was wont to sit, plying her needle, and occasionally rocking her infant's cradle with her foot, till, when twilight released her from her task, she stole out, in a thread-bare plaid gown—the best, indeed the only one she possessed—to dispose of her work, which seldom cleared more than sixpence after deducting for the materials. Small as the produce of her labours was, it was a little help, and she honestly declared she felt proud to add even that little to the industrious gains of " one of the best of husbands, fathers and men."

Early in October 1750, Strange left Paris for London, where in the following spring, he resolved to establish himself, hoping for better encouragement and a freer access to high class pictures than he could have looked for in Edinburgh. His wife gladly joined him, with her little girl, and they took up their residence in Parliament Street. At this time he commenced importing a number of pictures and engravings by the sale of which, as well as through his own works, he endeavoured to create a higher standard of taste. This object he never lost sight of, and it was in this manner that he rendered such eminent service to art. His first occupation, after his return, was to engrave some of the plates for an anatomical work of Dr. William Hunter; these drawings bear various dates; one of them was pronounced by Professor Simpson of Edinburgh, " as a mere work of art, perhaps the most beautiful anatomical plate ever given to the world." During the following year he devoted himself to more congenial labours, in preparing his two plates of the Magdalen and Cleopatra, both after Guido, the appearance of which procured him great reputation. No artist of eminence appears to have been more independent of extraneous aid than was Strange; and it is said that he occupied himself on the most mechanical parts of his plates rather than trust them to others; going to work with the dawn, the longest day being too short to fatigue his hand or exhaust his powers of application. In 1754, he removed to the Golden Head, in Henrietta Street, where he resided until 1762. There, in the spring of 1755, he published his admirable engraving of "Liberality and Modesty," in which the exquisite rendering of the flesh-texture is so remarkable. In accordance with the fashion of the time he produced as a companion print the "Apollo punishing Arrogance." This year was an eventful one in his domestic circle An infant son died of the small pox in May, and shortly after, Mrs. Strange was called to attend the sickbeds of her father and mother. In the course of the summer, Mrs. Lumisden died, and a twelve-month later her husband followed her to the grave. Another little one had meantime been added to the Strange family, and the fond mother of the young brood, thus described them in one of her letters to her still absent brother:—" My little Jamie was put into breeches last Sunday; he looks most charming; when he went into the park everybody called him the Young Chevalier. My little jewel Andrew, seems to have the finest ear for his age I ever knew. . . . . Mary Bruce (the eldest) seems to like writing best of any. She'll dance with a very graceful air; although she is far from possessing beauty, yet there is something agreeable about her, and she is very like her dear papa. Jamie is like me; he has a fine temper; but for Andrew, he truly is the most complete charmer I ever saw both in body and mind. His complexion is as brown as mine, and his eye as dark. God make them all good; you see I make them all bonny!" Another girl was born in 1759, "quite a Venus in miniature."

To maintain this numerous family, Strange was indefatigable in his profession. His biographer gives a list of the fifty principal works engraved by him during his laborious life, with their dates, and the prices at which they were sold. The latter were very low as compared to those of our day, the highest sum in no case amounting to a guinea. The proofs of his engravings, so highly prized by collectors, have since obtained large prices, amounting to £30 or £40, at various auctions.

In 1755 he made a journey to the Continent, the motives for which he thus announced in the introduction to his "Descriptive Catalogue" of 1769. "Having experienced the favour and protection of the public in the reception which they gave to several engravings which I executed after capital paintings of great masters, I resolved to undertake a journey into Italy, where I foresaw that I might be able to make such a collection of drawings as would furnish matter of still greater entertainment for the public, and would gratify that species of taste which I saw with great pleasure, was every day rising higher and diffusing itself further in this opulent country; and I flatter myself that my hopes have not been disappointed; I employed several years in travelling through and residing for some time in all the principal cities of Italy, where both in the churches and in the palaces of the great, I met with many excellent pictures, which appeared to me to be highly worthy of being made more generally known. In the execution of the drawings which I have made from these pictures, I had peculiar advantages, through the favour and munificence of several princes, and other considerable personages in Italy, and I exerted all the ability I was master of, insomuch that, if I have not vainly flattered myself, I have been happy enough even to preserve the peculiar character of each master, a circumstance essentially necessary in works of this nature."

With so many domestic cares to bind her to home, Mrs. Strange was obliged unwillingly to decline her brother's invitation, that she should accompany her husband abroad, and to reconcile herself to a lengthened interruption of her domestic happiness, for the sake of his professional prospects and the interests of her family. These advantages were, in some respects, dearly purchased. After seventeen years of married life, the attached couple could look back upon but about half that period as spent together, and to the peculiar temperament of the wife these prolonged absences were rendered more irksome by the increasing cares of a numerous family, and the complication of her father's affairs, which it became necessary she should superintend, as well as by the onerous duty of conducting the sale of her husband's works, without the intervention of any publisher.

Strange, at length wearied of long separations from his family, returned to London, and steadily continued for the next ten years labouring in the production of his numerous works; at the end of that time he carried his family with him to Paris, where they lived in the Rue d'Enfer for five years, and afterwards finally established themselves in Great Queen Street, Lincoln's Inn Fields. That which may be pronounced the master piece of his graver, his copy of Vandyke's Charles I. with the Duke of Hamilton, was published in 1782; in size, historical importance, and artistic merit none of his works exceeded it; the drapery is considered the most perfect of all he ever executed, and the landscape foreground, beyond all praise. A proof before the letter has fetched £22. Years were now multiplying upon the artist, and he had reached the height of his well-earned reputation. In 1787 he received the honour of knighthood; this event is related by his wife in a letter to their son Robert, dated January 13th, 1787.

"Your dear father has been employed in engraving a beautiful picture painted by Mr. West for his Majesty; it represents two of the royal children who died. The print was lately published, and Friday the 5th current was appointed for your father's presenting some proofs of it to the king. His majesty was very much pleased; after saying many most flattering things, he said, 'Mr. Strange, I have another favour to ask of you, it is that you will attend the levee on Wednesday or Friday that I may confer on you the honour of knighthood.' His majesty left the room, but coming quickly back, said, 'I'm going immediately to St. James's, if you'll follow me I will do it now; the sooner the better,' so calling one of the pages, gave him orders to conduct Mr. Strange to St. James's, where kneeling down, he rose up Sir Robert Strange. This honour to our family I hope is a very good omen. I hope it will be a spur to our children, and show them to what virtue and industry may bring them. Few families have ever had a more sure or creditable foundation than ours; may laurels flourish on all your heads!..."

From the pen of one of the family we have a pleasing sketch of Sir Robert in his waning years. "I was very happy with him," says his daughter-in-law's mother. "I never saw so pleasant and equal-tempered, agreeable man in my life, and so modest. His wife and he are the very opposite; for she is all fancy, fire and flash; yet very steady to the main chance; but he admires her, and is so well amused with her fancies, that, when silent, he starts a subject to make her shine. His works are amazing, and he has made engraving a source of wealth to the nation, as they now export prints to all parts of the world, to the value of £100,000. He recently had an illness; he thought himself dying, and had ordered his body to be carried to Orkney, where it seems he was born. His present plate is the Annunciation, and is superior to any he has done."

The shadows of evening now fast gathering around him, saw no relaxation of his self-imposed toil, and during the last five years of his life, six engravings were published by him in close succession. In January 1791, he quitted Paris for the last time. His health was failing, and a visit or two which he had made to the hot wells at Bristol, had not materially benefitted it. His devoted wife tended him with affectionate solicitude, while he arranged his affairs, including the selection of his choicest impressions for binding. In July 1792, he died, having attained the age of 71. His widow very touchingly describes his death in a letter to her son Andrew, concluding, —" Two days after he was put in a lead coffin, but I would not let it be closed for eight days. Often, often did I visit his dear cold face, kissed it, and knelt by him in that posture. I took the letters from my dear Bell (who had written, in ignorance of her father's death) and laid them on the breast of your dearest father, who could not feel the pain I did. There I prayed to the God of heaven, who made you, to guide and direct you in everything." Sir Robert was buried in a family tomb at the cemetery of St. Paul's, Covent Garden. In his will, dated 1789, he left to his children special legacies, amounting to £10,800, to his friend Benjamin West, P. R. A., a picture by A. Caracci; the residue of his fortune, including produce of his plates, prints, and pictures, was devised equally among his children.

Lady Strange, after surviving her husband fourteen years, died in 1806, in the 87th year of her age. Thirty-six years after the decease of this admirable woman, one of her daughters wrote of her, "Few women ever filled the duties of wife and mother equal to herself; I draw her character in these words,—she had beauty, wit, and good sense. How rarely are these three ever combined together in the same person!"

www.ingramcontent.com/pod-product-compliance
Lightning Source LLC
Chambersburg PA
CBHW030745230426
43667CB00007B/842